To Advance Learning

A Handbook on Developing K-12 Postsecondary Partnerships

Manuel N. Gomez
Joan Bissell
Lesley Danziger
Robin Casselman

With a foreword by John I. Goodlad

University Press of America
Lanham • New York • London

University Press of America®, Inc.
4720 Boston Way
Lanham, Maryland 20706

3 Henrietta Street
London WC2E 8LU England

Printed in the United States of America
British Cataloging in Publication Information Available

Co-published by arrangement with
Project STEP (Student/Teacher Education Partnership)
of the University of California, Irvine

Library of Congress Cataloging-in-Publication Data

To advance learning : a handbook on developing K–12/postsecondary
partnerships / Manuel N. Gomez ... [et al.].

p. cm.
Includes bibliographical references.
1. College–school cooperation–California–Case studies.
2. Project Student/Teacher Educational Partnership.
I. Gomez, Manuel N. II. Project Student/Teacher
Educational Partnership.
LB2331.53.T6 1990 378.1'03—dc20 90–42218 CIP

ISBN 0–8191–7942–6 (alk. paper)
ISBN 0–8191–7943–4 (pbk. : alk. Paper)

Project STEP: A Partnership for the Advancement of Learning

PROJECT STEP

STUDENT/TEACHER EDUCATIONAL PARTNERSHIP

Santa Ana Unified School District
Rancho Santiago College
California State University, Fullerton
University of California, Irvine

To the students of the Santa Ana Unified School District--may their learning prepare them for the challenges of the 21st Century.

Acknowledgements

School/college and university collaboration, by its very nature, implies the support and involvement of people from diverse institutions. This has been the case in our experience developing Project STEP. We are particularly grateful to the Carnegie Corporation of New York, the California Academic Partnership Program, and the College Board whose support has directly facilitated the development of Project STEP: A Partnership for the Advancement of Learning. This book was directly supported by a grant from the Carnegie Corporation of New York and the California Academic Partnership Program. The opinions expressed are those of the authors and do not necessarily reflect those of our sponsors.

We wish to acknowledge the many individuals who have been supportive of this partnership. First, we convey our heart-felt thanks to Gloria De Necochea, formerly of the Carnegie Corporation of New York, who first suggested this study and provided initial encouragement and support for the project. We wish to also express our deep appreciation to our friends with the Carnegie Corporation of New York. Our gratitude is extended to Karin Egan for her outstanding and continuing support of our work; to E. Alden Dunham for his leadership of the Education, Science, Teaching, and the Economy program; to Barbara Finberg for her support; and to Avery Russell for her special help. We, of course, are grateful to David Hamburg, president of the Carnegie Corporation of New York, for sharing his insights and generous comments regarding school/college collaboratives in the Prologue of this book.

We wish to also acknowledge and express our considerable appreciation to Deborah Hancock, the director of the California Academic Partnership Program, for her personal and financial support that enabled us to continue developing the STEP partnership model.

We thank all of the individuals who supported Project STEP in our affiliation with the College Board's EQ Models Program for School-College Collaboration. They include Adrienne Bailey, vice president for academic affairs; Eileen Bertsch, associate director of the Educational EQuality Project; Barbara Gombach; James Herbert and in particular, Paula Bagasao, both formerly with the College Board, for their early and continuing support. We thank Donald Stewart, president of the Board, for his comments provided in the Afterword of this book.

We benefited immensely from distinguished educational leaders and scholars who provided us with their critical suggestions and comments to earlier drafts of this study. They are Ed Apodaca, with the University of California, Office of the President, Berkeley, California; Gloria De Necochea of the ARCO Foundation, Los Angeles, California; Arturo Madrid, president of the Tomas Rivera Center in Claremont, California; Paula Bagasao, with the American Association of Higher Education, Washington, D.C.; Eileen Bertsch, of the College Board; Theodore Sizer, Brown University; Myron Atkin, Stanford University; and Dennis Galligani of the University of California, Irvine. John Goodlad, of the University of Washington, besides providing his comments in the Foreword, also contributed significantly with his willingness to share his views and ideas in our conversations regarding this handbook. We are grateful to all our reviewers for their insights, comments, and suggestions throughout each of the earlier stages of this study. They, of course, should not be held responsible for any of the authors' views or conclusions with which they may disagree.

We are especially indebted to the following individuals for the continuing development and success of Project STEP: Rudy Castruita, Superintendent of Santa Ana Unified School District; Jewel Plummer Cobb, President of California State University, Fullerton; Robert Jensen, Chancellor of Rancho Santiago College; and Jack Peltason, Chancellor of the University of California, Irvine. We appreciate their support and involvement in Project STEP.

It is impossible to list all of the individuals who have participated from Santa Ana Unified School District and the postsecondary partners. The chronology in Appendix A mentions many colleagues who have through the years contributed toward this project and provides a roster of the STEP Administrative Council membership and STEP Component coordinators. We extend our special thanks to all the individuals with the Santa Ana Unified School District including the Board of Education, District staff, the high school, intermediate school, and elementary school principals, and all of the teachers, students, and parents, who have contributed with their ongoing participation to the success of this partnership.

How does one thank one's own partners? Words begin to fall short. We wish to express our very special appreciation to Anna Manring for her enduring patience with all of us, her outstanding skill in typesetting the manuscript, and her distinct ability to simply smile at our endless reviews and inevitable edits.

The entire EOP/SAA staff of the University of California, Irvine deserves a special thanks for building the foundation upon which Project STEP is developing. My personal thanks to my secretary, Bev Pirtle, who struggled valiantly to assist me in meeting crucial deadlines and providing the essential administrative support that greatly facilitated the completion of this work.

Words cannot convey my deep gratitude for my friends and co-authors, Joan Bissell, Lesley Danziger, and Robin Casselman. Without them, this book simply would not have been.

My wife, Genet, and our children, Maya and Tomas, deserve more than I can ever express for their wonderful love, patience, and understanding.

M.N.G.
Santa Ana, California
April, 1990

CONTENTS

Foreword

More than a decade ago, I wrote a letter to eighteen school superintendents in southern California addressing the degree to which educational problems of the time were overwhelming the ability of any given institution to deal with them adequately. I then proceeded to list a dozen or so such problems, all of which had been regarded and still were being regarded as part of the turf occupied by schools or universities but rarely both. I suggested that they be addressed in concert.

My colleagues and I were engaged at the time in a comprehensive study of schooling in the United States from which emerged ultimately thirty-five technical reports, a clutch of articles in professional journals, and five books. The study had emerged out of a project embracing eighteen schools, the League of Cooperating Schools, emphasizing processes of change. Through these processes we had discovered very stubborn problems which I came to call later "hard rock problems." We decided that we needed to get a better handle on them and so embarked on the study mentioned above. In examining the data beginning to come together late in that decade, I realized that we had been on the right track in the work embracing the League of Cooperating Schools but that the strategy had to be expanded to involve not just a clutch of schools but also the larger educational structure of which schools are a part and the university. Hence my letter to the eighteen school superintendents.

Most of the superintendents accepted the invitation to join me for lunch and discussion. There was general agreement that the problems were highly resistant to attack and that chances for success would be strengthened if the unique resources of the university were added to those of the schools. We formed a collaboration between the Laboratory for School and Community Education of the Graduate School of Education at UCLA and school districts in four counties. We were ambitious enough at that time to include a number of community colleges receiving the graduates of these schools and sending some of them to the University of California.

This was the first of the partnerships that ultimately came to constitute the present National Network for Educational Renewal. As word of The Partnership began to get around, inquiries regarding the creation of similar structures elsewhere began to come in. One of the most serious of these came from the College of Education of Brigham Young University in Utah. Out of that inquiry and a subsequent invitation came the BYU-Public School Partnership.

In 1985, those of us in the Laboratory who had been most closely connected with The Partnership scattered to assume positions in states separated by a good deal of terrain: California, Maine, and Washington. Our interests in school-university partnerships continued.

At the University of Washington, I extended my thinking to a concept of symbiotic school-university partnerships through which two quite different cultures (schools and universities) came together because they have mutually overlapping self-interests and because each will satisfy its own self-interests and those of the other partners better through collaboration. Simultaneously, an interest of administrators in several school districts discussed with several of us at the University of Washington, led to creation of the Puget Sound Educational Consortium. The inquiries kept coming in, and by April 1986, we were able to announce that the National Network for Educational Renewal consisted of fourteen school-university partnerships in as many states.

One of the fundamental ideas behind symbiotic school-university partnerships is that there will be a common agenda--that is, schools and a partner university will work together on the same problems, problems which have been worked on separately before the partnership was entered into. The partners are equal. That is, each has an equal voice whether the problem traditionally has been embraced primarily or exclusively by the university or the schools. Consequently, reform in programs for the preparation of school principals is as open to full participation on the part of school people as it is to university people. Similarly, university people have an equal voice in addressing problems traditionally dealt with by schools alone.

This kind of joining is not easy. Indeed, it is so difficult that, at times, the dynamics of creating a collaborative process often obfuscate the nature of the problem being addressed. University people are accustomed to bringing their expertise to the schools, usually as consultants. The reverse rarely has been the case. Consequently, university people have a great deal of difficulty at first in recognizing school people as equal partners and, indeed, letting them into their territory at all. School people on the other hand do not always trust those from the university. They often believe, rightly, that the latter are there to gather data for a paper to be published in a professional journal.

My colleagues and I have now been at the business of creating and advancing the idea of school-university partnerships for over a decade. We have learned a great deal, some of which has been expressed in our occasional paper series, and Kenneth Sirotnik and I even ventured to edit a book of papers on the subject, ***School-University Partnerships in Action*** (Teachers College Press 1988). There is much more to learn. Recently, at a meeting in Chicago, executive directors of the partnerships came together to recommit themselves to the concepts and to continued membership in the National Network for Educational Renewal. School-university partnerships appear to be an idea whose time is come.

In southern California, The Partnership referred to above (now embracing the Claremont Graduate School rather than UCLA as the university partner) is not the only example of close school-university collaboration. For example, Project STEP embraces the University of California, Irvine, the Santa Ana Unified School District, California State University (Fullerton), and Rancho Santiago Community College. As the Introduction to this Handbook states, Project STEP began at the University of California, Irvine, in 1983. Its scope of activity has grown enormously during the intervening years. Today, it is a vital, vibrant demonstration of the degree to which institutions of higher education, when those connected with them have the will to do so, can contribute significantly to the educational health of children and youths in surrounding schools. We take it for granted that the university-based health sciences will contribute to the educational health of the community, but there has not been a strong parallel conception with respect to the role of the university in the educational health of the community. Once upon a time in our history, the relationship between higher education and the elementary and secondary schools was much more clearly seen and, in my judgment, much better. Institutions of higher education not yet involved in activities similar to those embraced by Project STEP must come to do so if the educational system we have long sought is to come into being.

As is pointed out early on in this significant document, the next step for Project STEP is for school people to become more intimately involved with the traditionally campus-bound programs of preparing educators for the schools. A program for the preparation of school principals, for example, becomes much stronger when it is enlightened and, in part, conducted by practitioners who are themselves models of sound educational practices. This connection should be recognized as natural. But things appearing to be natural often are not.

Clearly, we are not going to get better teachers for the schools until they have better school settings in which to gain the practice part of their preparatory experiences. Today, we prepare teachers magnificently for the schools we have. We need to be preparing teachers for schools that are better than those we now have and so universities and school districts must work together in designing these exemplary sites. This will not be easy. We are going into the final decade of the twentieth century after a sustained period of attempting to reform our schools. Some good things have happened but much more remains to be done. Improving schools is very difficult. Improving schools and teacher education simultaneously is even more difficult--but this is what we must do.

Project STEP represents a giant leap forward in the right direction. But the road ahead is longer and more difficult than the road already behind. This road will be traveled most successfully to the degree that the collaborating schools and institutions of higher education are joined in a symbiotic school-university partnership.

John I. Goodlad
March 1990

Prologue

The decade of the 1980s has been characterized by reports critical of American education, especially elementary and secondary. The decade of the 1990s may well be characterized by extensive restructuring of American education. One element of such restructuring involves partnerships between schools and other institutions that can enrich pre-collegiate education. Among such partnerships, none is more promising than those involving schools and universities.

The purpose of this study is not to urge the adoption of a single structure for school/university partnerships, but rather to report on one outstanding collaboration. This project provides one valuable model from which educational leaders may learn important lessons as they establish their own cooperative relationships within their local contexts. It testifies to the vitality of the rapidly developing partnership movement that is one response to the school reform ferment of the past decade.

If we are serious about transforming the quality of our schooling across the educational continuum from K-12 to graduate study, it will require a much greater degree of substantive cooperation between schools and universities than has been the case so far. In order to upgrade the teaching profession, we must address the professional work experience of teachers. One promising path for enhancing the teaching profession is to support mutually beneficial relationships between K-12 and higher education faculty--to provide a forum, for example, that permits teachers to work together in addressing specific curricular concerns within their discipline. Project STEP has been noteworthy in achieving this result.

An important and appealing aspect of these genuinely collaborative strategies is that they provide an opportunity to move away from the piecemeal approaches to addressing the many needs facing American education. If we can strengthen the capacity to address these needs with a comprehensive approach such as Project STEP incorporates, I believe we can accelerate progress in this field.

Project STEP has been characterized by a sense of excitement regarding the wide range of opportunities for collaboration between schools and universities. Its leaders have built the program in a way that fosters sustained cooperation rather than a quick fix. We need more educational architects to construct such essential bridges between schools and universities. Manuel Gomez and his colleagues deserve our respect for the excellent work reflected in this stimulating innovation.

The Carnegie Corporation of New York has made a major investment in support of collaborative programs to strengthen the relationships between schools, colleges, and universities. The linking of schools with institutions of higher education--as well as with the business and corporate community--offers a viable strategy for implementing substantial reforms in American education on a nation-wide basis. Such partnerships have special promise for disadvantaged minority education, since they can strengthen schools otherwise vulnerable in poor communities.

Partnerships offer the opportunity to strengthen connections between research and actual classroom teaching practices. Both assessment of good practices and school-based research are essential for guiding long-term improvement of education. Partnerships can bring together faculty at different levels within the educational system to develop new knowledge and skills leading to improved practices. Collaboration provides the opportunity for K-12 educators to assume the leadership in partnerships with university faculty to reform their own schools. Such relationships can overcome insularity and stereotypes. They move us toward a coherent, unified educational community.

Project STEP is enhancing the essential democratic processes within our public schools by experimenting with the development of new consensual governance structures and procedures for educational institutions. It has created conditions in which educational personnel, students, and parents can work together toward important school improvement.

Particularly noteworthy is the fact that the percentage of students going on to higher education has increased from ten percent to sixty-five percent since Project STEP was established. This is in a district that is composed of 92% ethnic-minority students. Higher education institutions must pay attention to demographic trends. If they want excellent students in the next decade, they must help in their preparation and reach out to those who are at an early disadvantage.

By establishing long-term collaborative relations between schools and universities, by sharing human resources, partnerships can provide exceptional leadership in the vital upgrading of education.

David A. Hamburg, M.D.
President
Carnegie Corporation of New York

Introduction

> *Let all divisions of knowledge be accepted rather for lines and veins, than for sections and separations, and the continuance and entireness of knowledge be preserved.* (Francis Bacon, ***The Advancement of Learning,*** 1605).

To a large extent there are few existing direct linkages between the K-12 and the postsecondary sector, except for the students who pass from one to the other. However, there has been renewed interest in recent years in the many advantages of linking these two sectors of education. These linkages take on a variety of forms: networks, collaborations and cooperative ventures of all levels of impact. Some focus on staff development of secondary faculty; some focus on curriculum articulation; some focus on early entry and bridge programs for students. Often, relationships between the two educational sectors are hierarchical, with the college sector offering its "expertise" to the K-12 educators. Historically, these two sectors have been guided by very different cultures, which have had little positive effect on each other. Differences in the "two cultures" are manifested in different administrative structures, and different values regarding research and pedagogy.

Project STEP offers a model for using the partnership approach to bridge these two cultures and to reduce the hierarchical relationships that have impeded educational cooperatives in general and other partnership efforts in particular. In this partnership, the educators in the K-12 school district and in the postsecondary institutions in its proximity work together to improve many aspects of educational performance. As described by Odell and Mock in ***A Crucial Agenda,***

> Project STEP represents a significant effort to reconstruct the relationships among all segments of education in order to improve academic preparation for . . . students. What makes STEP unusual is the level of interinstitutional cooperation between the school district, community college and four year colleges and universities involved (Odell and Mock 1989, 108).

The partnership is effecting positive change in the structure of relationships between and within partnership institutions. For example, in Faculty Forums, faculty from all sectors share ideas on pedagogy and research. Moreover, the STEP administrative framework of shared governance and coequal participation encourages a new level of equity and professionalism not only in relations between educators but between educators and administrators. This cultural change in values and assumptions is the most difficult goal for partnerships and other collaboratives to achieve.

Project STEP is unusual in the extent as well as the depth of collaboration that it has developed between the partnership institutions. A complex set of partnership activities includes three broad areas of focus: (1) a wide array of interdisciplinary and discipline-specific curriculum revision projects, especially in the areas of Mathematics, Science and Language Arts; (2) faculty development and preservice programs for improved preparation for teaching, particularly with regard to students in multicultural and multilingual classrooms; and (3) a comprehensive and continuous system of support and curricular guidance for students in the secondary schools.

STEP initiatives have also provided parents with greater access to information about the education of their children and with programs that help them reinforce education in the home, beginning at the elementary school level. It is opening the collaboration to include the business sector as an important additional resource of ideas and career guidance.

The STEP concept originated in the University of California, Irvine (UCI) Educational Opportunity Program/Student Affirmative Action--Outreach Office, and was initially developed as a partnership between the University of California at Irvine and the Santa Ana Unified School District. In 1983 the first STEP Faculty Forums were held between these faculties; and in July 1984 the first formal STEP Administrative Council meeting was held, with representatives from four partner institutions, expanded to include Rancho Santiago Community College and California State University at Fullerton. What began as a traditional "service model" relationship between the university and the district has evolved to a multifaceted, reciprocal partnership with many benefits for the K-12 district and the three postsecondary institutions

The partnership has achieved significant success in raising the academic aspirations and achievements of students in the Santa Ana Unified School District--presently 92% ethnic "minority." When the partnership began in 1983, the Santa Ana district already had the largest population of minority/low income students in Orange County (84%). Statistics revealed an atmosphere of low academic achievement and low student aspirations, particularly with regard to continuing education to the postsecondary sector. According to a survey conducted by the UCI Early Outreach Partnership Program the same year, only 6% of the district's minority students were enrolled in college preparatory classes; district surveys reported only 12% of the graduates planning to continue their education at the postsecondary level.

Annual district surveys since then have indicated a dramatic increase in higher education expectations on the part of administrators and faculty as well as students: administrators have increased the numbers of class sections offered in higher level mathematics and science classes; faculty have encouraged increased student participation in PSAT/SAT scholastic achievement test programs; and students have increased their postsecondary enrollment. Over 90% of the participants in the UCI Early Outreach Partnership Program now enroll in college preparatory classes, and 65% of the district's high school graduates surveyed are going on to further education.

This progress can largely be attributed to the partnership, which has focused overall partnership goals on student academic advancement, particularly in the areas of mathematics, science, and language arts, with special reference to the large number of language minority students enrolled in the school district. But accomplishments such as these are not the result of one simple strategy or program. The educators who have joined efforts in Project STEP perceive academic advancement to be a complex process. Part of this process includes joint curriculum review and enhancement with corresponding faculty development programs. Another part of this process includes building academic support programs for students, improving access for parental involvement, and fostering student interest in career planning and exploration, such as in the teaching profession. Hence, the partnership addresses all of these areas through a matrix of interrelated activities, which is highly organized but at the same time autonomous and flexible according to changing needs, and governed by a high degree of communication and trust between partnership constituents.

Clearly, Project STEP was designed to address the particular needs of a K-12 institution composed primarily of minority students, with the goal of providing quality education to all of its students. However, since so-called minority groups will comprise the majority of the population of California and one-third of the entire U.S. population by the year 2000, there is much to be learned by all educators from both the general framework and the specific components of the STEP partnership.

This handbook presents a model for school/college partnerships to utilize and expand upon. It outlines the history of Project STEP and analyzes the specific elements that have contributed to Project STEP's early success and its ongoing durability. Lessons are derived directly from the STEP experience and supported by reference to the emerging literature on academic partnerships. Sections focus on the following:

- how the literature defines "partnership" and other forms of cooperation and collaboration;

- how to structure and develop a partnership, given a particular context and an underlying assumption of the need for equity in interinstitutional relationships;

- how to define shared goals, resolve conflicting goals, and develop specific objectives and collaborative strategies to advance learning;

- how to establish a core administrative team, and identify and secure needed fiscal and human resources;

- how to develop student academic support programs and build parental involvement;

- how to achieve meaningful involvement of all constituency groups and participants;

- how to evaluate partnership efforts, and communicate effectively for both internal and external purposes; and

- how to sustain partnership leadership and momentum, despite very different "cultures" and relationships within the different institutions.

In presenting the Project STEP model, this book attempts not only to analyze the specific elements that can contribute to a partnership's success, but also to highlight strategies to cope with the problems and hurdles that interinstitutional partnerships face and the mistakes that they may make. Project STEP is a partnership that has achieved much, but is still evolving and has much to learn. Hopefully, in contributing to the emerging network of partnerships in the nation, we will learn from each other.

CHAPTER 1

The Organizational Features and Structure of an Effective Intersegmental Partnership

The world seems mad in preoccupation with what is specific, particular, disconnected (John Dewey 1916).

- *Defining partnerships*
- *The experience of Project STEP*
- *The governance of school-college collaboratives*
- *Positive outcomes of a collaborative approach*
- *A checklist of key organizational characteristics*

THIS CHAPTER will discuss the organizational features and structure that have contributed to the effectiveness of the Project STEP "Student/Teacher Educational Partnership." There are many models of intersegmental cooperation and collaboration; partnerships, according to many theorists, present the most challenging undertaking. A useful basis for comparison of the differing models is their responsiveness to the generally accepted premise that the K-12 schools and the postsecondary colleges and universities operate from entirely different cultures. Project STEP's response to this basic premise will be discussed in the context of the variety of school/college relationships currently in practice. A closer analysis of STEP's response to the particular cultures within its partnership will be presented in Chapter 9, *Sustaining Leadership and Momentum.*

Defining Partnerships

Two Cultures

In describing the K-12 and the postsecondary sector in terms of two cultures, most theorists highlight the differences in values and assumptions between the two in terms of research and pedagogy. These differences have led to a significant lack of understanding and distrust between the two sectors, as each culture has tended to distrust the value of the other's emphasis (Lieberman 1986, Sarason 1977, Haberman 1971). The two cultures are also reflected in differences between administrative procedures and style, in differences dealing with control, policy-making, public criticism and expenditures of funds (Lortie 1977, Wu 1985). Wilbur refers to the difference in organizational climate between the college and the K-12 schools. He uses the terminology "cool vs. intense" to describe this difference:

> University faculty members generally have intermittent teaching assignments; they often have private office space, time and facilities to do research; and they have considerable control over their daily schedules. Public high school teachers, on the other hand, usually have their work day booked to capacity, have almost no private space, and seldom have opportunity for planning and research. Problems of communication between the two often stem from differences in their professional environment (Wilbur 1981, 39).

Given that educational institutions recognize this fundamental difference in culture, what type of relationship can they develop with each other? Sadly, of course, many institutions choose to develop no relationship, on the assumption, presumably, that avoidance is the best response to a conflict of values. However, given a specific need, or problem, institutions that are fundamentally different are more likely to enter into a cooperative or collaborative mode. At this point, the relationship can take on different perspectives, according to the perception of the "ownership" of the problem or need, and the extent to which the institutions are prepared to impact each other's cultures.

Networks

Networking describe the relationships between individuals or institutions who share the same culture. Within a networking relationship, these individuals can exchange information, strategies and resources to deal with problems and needs that they share. There are a variety of examples of networks which have been facilitated by universities or colleges, but which primarily involve interaction between members of the K-12 sector and respond to the needs of that sector. Clark refers, for example, to the Metropolitan School Study Council, which is composed of a large number of school districts (forty-six, as of 1986) and Teachers College, Columbia University (Clark 1986, 43).

Cooperatives

Cooperatives refer to relationships that are instituted when schools from the K-12 sector and the postsecondary sector help each other to address separate goals. Hord (1986) presents a review of the differences cited between the cooperative and collaborative models. Basically, the cooperative has many attributes, but it focuses usually on one culture's area of need (the K-12 sector) and is often hierarchical in nature. Universities and colleges are more likely to view their participation in cooperatives as a "service" rather than an opportunity for self-improvement (Goodlad 1985, 1986).

Collaboration

Collaboration involves a fairly giant step beyond the cooperative mode. In a collaborative relationship, the K-12 and postsecondary institutions work together, as equals, to achieve mutual goals. Collaborations offer *each other* products or services (Hord 1986). Their organizational features are characterized by shared decision-making, open and frequent communication, exchange of resources, and consensus on educational goals. Clark refers to the following definition of collaborations as representative of the general tone of the literature:

> [Collaboration:] shared decision-making in governance, planning, delivery, and evaluation of programs. It is a pluralistic form of education where people of

> dissimilar backgrounds work together with equal status. It may be seen as working with rather than working on a person (Clark 1986, 40).

Inevitably, both K-12 and postsecondary cultures are significantly impacted by a collaborative relationship. The rewards are significant but impediments to collaboration are manifold. Apart from overcoming the problems of collaborating across cultures, collaborations face problems such as lack of personnel, time and financial support.

Partnerships

Partnerships represent a particular form of collaboration. John Goodlad stresses the importance of the "symbiotic" nature of partnerships. The key aspect of symbiosis in this context is the idea of "mutual satisfaction of self-interests" (Goodlad 1988, 14). For Goodlad, the main failing of many partnerships has been the incapacity or unwillingness on the part of the postsecondary sector to demonstrate the benefits of its interaction with the K-12 sector, especially in terms of improved education of teachers. Clark quotes Goodlad on this point:

> The argument for school-university partnerships proceeds somewhat as follows. For schools to get better, they must have better teachers, among other things. To prepare better teachers (and counselors, special educators and administrators), universities must have access to schools using the best practices. To have the best practices, schools need access to new ideas and knowledge. This means that universities have a stake in school improvement just as schools have a stake in the education of teachers (Clark 1986, 6).

The Experience of Project Step

Project STEP is an evolving model of an intersegmental partnership. It is a partnership which has put a premium on equality of relations, on sensitivity to the needs and goals of each participating institution, and on developing shared goals to which each institution can contribute. A significant question that guided the early development of the partnership was:

> to what extent can an intersegmental model of collaboration between a secondary school district and postsecondary institutions develop new incentives to create an environment where academic excellence will grow? (Gomez 1983, 5).

This growth in academic excellence has been and continues to be achieved by the students and faculties involved in Project STEP largely because of its adherence to the principles of collaboration and true partnerships that we have indicated. The basic principles and organizational features of Project STEP reveal an emphasis on the importance of shared governance, equity and reciprocity of benefits in the relationships between the educational sectors. The array of Project STEP components also reveals the partnership's understanding that the attainment of academic excellence for all students is necessarily a comprehensive venture, encompassing all aspects of the student's educational experience, including the support and understanding of his or her family.

Basic Principles

Project STEP's structure, like that of other successful partnerships, is directly linked to the needs, interests and resources of the specific partners and to the basic principles which guided the actions of the project originators. After researching and studying governance structures, Gordon B. Van de Water concluded that "the best governance structure is the one that fits the history and context of a particular situation" (Van de Water 1989, 25).

The four basic assumptions that emerged early as guiding principles of Project STEP are as follows:

- the conviction that collaboration involving each sector in the entire educational continuum and including faculty, staff, students and parents can advance more effective learning;

- the belief that a comprehensive scope of activities across the curricular spectrum holds the key to school-based reform;

- the certainty that higher education should cooperate with secondary schools for a reciprocal channeling of a variety of resources to improve teaching and learning;

- the recognition that institutionalization is fostered through the development of a an organizational structure which includes the participation of the chief executive officers.

Although the conventional wisdom is to focus on a narrow area of intervention, the Project STEP partnership, given the initial needs of the district and mutual concerns of the postsecondary partner institutions, designed a set of components which included a broad range of discipline-specific faculty development programs as well as student support programs. Each component was designated under the lead responsibility of one of the partner institutions, assuring that each partner had a "stake" in the collaborative. Part of the success of the Project STEP partnership can be attributed to this scope of activity paired with a managerial structure that fostered shared governance as a means of administering and coordinating multiple project components.

Key Organizational Features of Project STEP

The key organizational features and attributes of Project STEP--which have contributed significantly to its success as an effective intersegmental partnership--reflect many of the theoretical characteristics of a successful collaborative described in the relevant literature. They emphasize the ideas of equity, coequal participation, and shared decision-making. The project operates on the premise that change will not occur unless all partnership participants, from the chief executive officers and senior administrators to all school site personnel, have the opportunity to engage in the decision-making processes and leadership roles of the partnership. Specific features of the STEP partnership have been that:

- **Long-term commitment** from the university, college, district and school-site leaders, based on individual and shared long-term goals, assures that the partnership experiences will sustain multi-agency administrative support;

- The organizational structure of the project, in particular its **Administrative Council**, with high level representatives of the four participating institutions, provides a foundation for fostering and sustaining cooperation sufficiently strong to overcome organizational pressures that might otherwise serve as impediments to major reform.

- **Shared governance** is practiced, in which leadership is exerted by district and school site staff *in collaboration* with institutions of higher learning and in support of the goals of all participating institutions. Often intersegmental partnerships collapse because they fail to work with the school district's curricular, guidance and other goals. Project STEP began as an outgrowth of UC Irvine's Early Academic Outreach program. Because of this genesis, university dominance of Project STEP might have occurred. Over time, UC Irvine staff have increasingly limited their visible leadership in favor of promoting district and school site leadership.

- **Coequal participation has been characteristic of the development of the project component programs.** Each partner institution takes lead responsibility for the specific design, implementation, and follow-through of one or more of the "STEP Components."

- **The Teacher Advisory Committee** provides an effective administrative voice to participating teachers, thus ensuring responsiveness to school-site initiatives.

- **A comprehensive scope** has been defined which addresses three broad interdependent objectives: curriculum enhancement, professional development, and student academic support. Project STEP's program components respond to each of these areas.

- **A focused action plan has been developed which is aligned with long-term institutional goals.** It has clear goals and measurable objectives, and includes mechanisms for communication, teamwork, and ongoing evaluation. Project STEP examined the potential interfaces among the long-term goals of each partner institution before devising a program of specific components which form an integrated matrix of support for students, faculty, parents and counselors. A strong commitment to evaluation is integral to the project, accompanied by the ongoing use of evaluation results. The STEP Data Evaluation Committee is a formalized entity having responsibility for coordinating all the reporting of evaluation results for the partnership.

- **Adequate resources** are committed to the support of cross-segmental activities such as curriculum revision teamwork by postsecondary and secondary staffs. This includes the channeling of funding sources which also bring the Project STEP partnership into a wider network of collaborative activities. Current funding sources include: the California Academic Partnership Program (CAPP), the Carnegie Corporation of New York, and the College Board's Educational EQuality Project Models Program for School-College Collaboration. Each of the participating partner institutions have also contributed significant resources. (See Appendix B for *Select Projects and Organizations Which Support Collaborative and Partnership Efforts.*)

It should be noted additionally that stability has been a characteristic of many of Project STEP's key administrative positions. Project STEP has been fortunate to retain the same Project Director and Associate Director since its inception. This continuity of leadership has been important since, as is to be expected, there have been changes in other key personnel within the school district and the postsecondary sectors.

Project STEP's Organizational Structure

The Administrative Council

The chief decision-making body of the Project STEP partnership is the Administrative Council. The Administrative Council is composed of representatives of the four institutions which comprise Project STEP. They are appointed to three-year terms by the chief executive officers of each partner institution.

The Administrative Council has two main functions: First, it allows many of the key leaders at the school district, college and university sites to participate in the overall planning of the partnership. For example, at one STEP Administrative Council meeting, the council was comprised of the following range of participants: eleven postsecondary faculty and administrators, eleven principals, five senior school district administrators, the district superintendent and the school district's teachers association representative. Second, it coordinates the multiple components of the partnership to insure that they reinforce current and long-term goals of the collaboration. In doing so, it allows the partnership institutions to brainstorm approaches and resources in the development of new components. The Administrative Council will be described in greater detail in Chapter Three.

The Data Evaluation and Teacher Advisory Committee

Two other formalized committees, the Data Evaluation Committee and the Teacher Advisory Committee, provide input for decision-making by the Administrative Council.

(1) *The Data Evaluation Committee* provides the partnership with assessment instruments, evaluation of specific project component activities, information about student participation, and performance

data about the project, reflecting outcomes at both the K-12 and postsecondary levels. (2) *The Teacher Advisory Committee* elects one member to serve on the Administrative Council. It provides input from District teachers to the Administrative Council; it also communicates information regarding STEP initiatives and programs to other faculty throughout the district.

The Project Components and Associated Task Forces

Over the seven-year history of Project STEP, there have been three major phases of organizational arrangements, all based on the same fundamental structure: STEP has been focused on one K-12 school district, non-hierarchical in its governance approach utilizing the STEP Administrative Council to oversee all partnership functions, and comprehensive both in the scope of its participants and in the range of collaborative activities sponsored by the partner institutions. Typically, the project activities have been coordinated through seven to ten STEP Components, with corollary ad hoc committees and/or formal task forces supporting these efforts.

For example, under the initial phase of Project STEP as a "Model of Intersegmental Collaboration" from January 1985 through June 1987, the following components were designed and implemented by the partner institutions:

- Critical Thinking/Reading: CSUF
- Critical Thinking/Writing: UCI
- Mathematics/Science Curriculum Development: UCI
- Faculty Forums: Joint/STEP Council
- Tutorial Services: RSC
- Instructional Guidance/ Student Progress Monitoring: SAUSD/UCI
- Parents in Partnership: UCI

PROJECT STEP

Organization Chart

(1988-89)

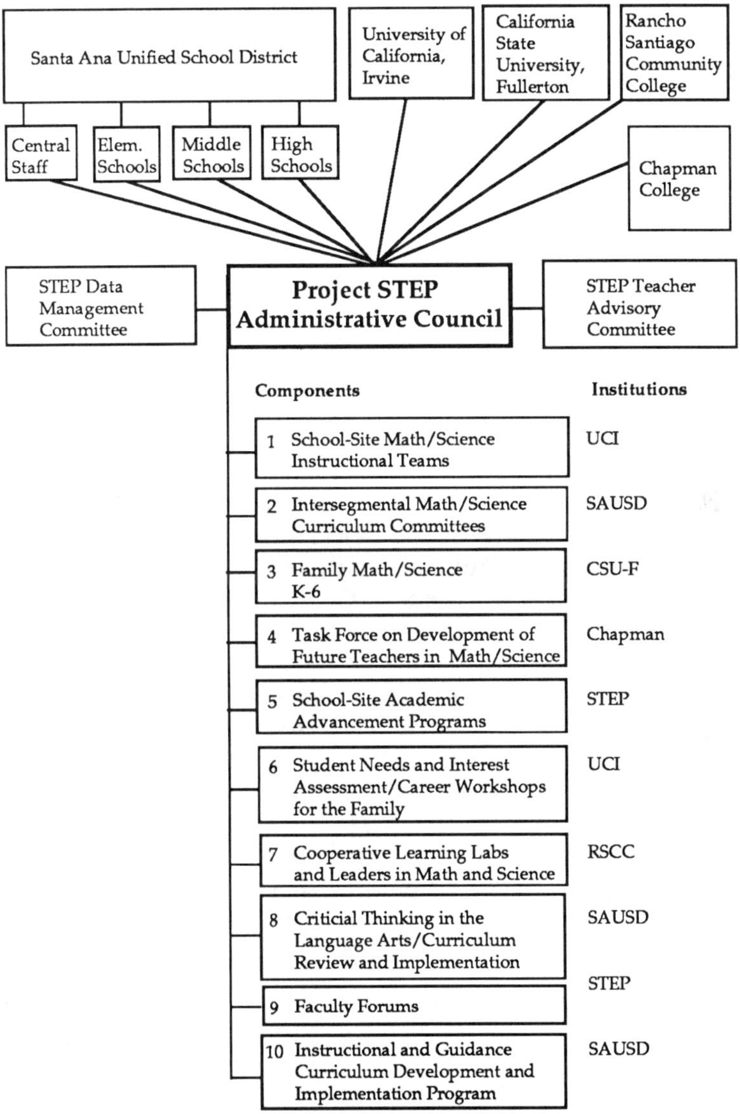

On the basis of assessments of the partnership's needs and resources in the fall of 1986, three main areas were targeted for action during the period from July 1987 through June 1990: (1) Mathematics and Science Academic Preparation; (2) Student Academic Support and Future Teacher Recruitment; and (3) Faculty Forums/Professional Development. These areas were further broken down into ten components.

Generally, these STEP components, identified in the organizational chart displayed on page 11, are the responsibility of one of the participating institutions. However, task forces formed under the leadership of an institution to develop a component will typically be drawn from most or all partnership institutions. This system of components and the emphasis on coequal participation in the development of component segments provides an opportunity for ongoing collaboration across all educational segments and levels. Component activities are discussed in greater detail in Chapter Five, *Achieving Meaningful Involvement of All Constituency Groups.*

The Governance of School-College Collaboratives: Van de Water

In *The Governance of School-College Collaboratives: Lessons Learned from the College Board's Educational Equality Project Models Program for School-College Collaboration,* written for The College Board in 1989, Gordon B. Van de Water summarizes the governance characteristics of successful collaboratives referred to in the literature by many of the current writers (J. Goodlad, K. Sirotnik, J. Vivian, F. Wilbur, B. Gifford, A. Bailey, D. Galligani, D. Martin, et al):

> *1. Mutual self-interest and common goals.* A clearly articulated and accepted statement of mutual self-interest and common goals appears to be a necessary starting point for building a successful collaborative. While the various parties to a collaborative effort may have personal or institutional interests in participating, it is important that they identify and agree on a common focus for the effort and understand how each will gain from the commitment.

2. ***Mutual trust and respect.*** Collaborative activities must develop mutual trust and respect among members. Each participant must understand the unique experience and perspective that others bring to the collaborative and demonstrate a willingness to work together on a professional basis.

3. ***Shared decision-making.*** Successful collaboratives stress the involvement of all parties in decision-making. Whether the issue is the focus of collaborative activity, the approach to be used, the allocation of resources, or the evaluation of results, it is important that collaborative members share decision-making responsibility.

4. ***Clear focus.*** Given the many complex issues that could be addressed, it is important to establish a clear focus. The Yale-New Haven Teachers Institute's experience is instructive: "One of the most persistent issues for the Institute is keeping our work sharply focused where the need is compelling."

5. ***Manageable agenda.*** A corollary to establishing a clear focus is the need to spell out a meaningful agenda and focus activities in accordance with this agenda. Because resources--both time and money--will always be limited, collaborative members must discipline themselves when setting their mutual agenda and implementing cooperative ventures. Being focused and keeping the organizational elements both solid and straightforward appear to work best.

6. ***Commitment from top leadership.*** Because collaboration is often seen initially as peripheral to core functions, it is necessary to have both the commitment and involvement of top leaders from each of the participating entities. Leaders provide legitimacy to the undertaking, underscore its importance, and have the capacity to commit resources.

7. Fiscal support. Adequate fiscal support is not only important to cover the costs of collaboration, it is also critical to the collaborative activity being taken seriously. When scarce resources are allocated to an activity, the message is clear that the leadership considers the activity important and worthy of financial investment.

8. Long-term commitment. Changing the way that schools and colleges work together to address complicated issues requires years of patient work. Participants in collaboratives should understand that results are not likely to be immediate. Change will be slow and outcomes difficult to evaluate in the short term. The long-term outcomes will be seen in institutional as well as programmatic change. The commitment to sustained collaboration must be made firmly by K-12 and postsecondary participants in order for change to be significant and lasting.

9. Dynamic nature. Collaborative activity typically begins with a shared understanding of the problem(s). As experience is gained, some avenues are found to be more fruitful than others. This dynamic development of collaborative activities should be recognized as normal and should be encouraged.

10. Information sharing. Because members of collaboratives typically have other full-time professional commitments, it is particularly important to ensure that all members are kept informed. Contact with other collaborative models also insures constant input of information and ideas to modify and enrich the partnership. (Van de Water, 1989, 3.)

Positive Consequences of Project STEP's Organizational Features and Structure

The Project STEP Administrative Council, as its first task in the summer of 1984, deliberated on a Statement of Purpose and Structure. An organizational structure based on the principles of shared governance, open communication and coequal participation was developed.

SCHOOL DISTRICT LEADERS have generally welcomed the STEP collaboration as a two-way learning vehicle. Administrators of the Santa Ana Unified School District do not perceive themselves as primarily "serving as a laboratory" for the postsecondary institutions in their partnership; rather, Project STEP has become integral to district goals--a vehicle for furthering the realization of significant objectives on the part of the district itself. As school and district staff have become aware of the resources available through STEP and their own ability to shape these resources in ways appropriate to their local needs, they have generated and implemented new initiatives and additional collaborative projects. The most current example of such initiatives is the district's leadership in establishing STEP Task Forces in the key areas of (1) science and technology education; (2) drug abuse prevention; (3) student outreach; (4) future teacher recruitment; (5) faculty forums; and (6) mathematics. Dr. Rudy Castruita, Superintendent of the Santa Ana Unified School District, notes:

> As I travel around the nation to attend various forums and share some lessons from our Project STEP model, I am continually surprised to learn how unique our collaborative experience is. The Santa Ana District now routinely responds to educational concerns through a cooperative strategy that directly engages our postsecondary partners.

TEACHERS experience a greater sense of professionalism and commitment as they influence the project and perform leadership roles. One of the benefits of a project such as this is the genuine leadership of teachers and their commitment in their work with students and parents to improving the quality of education that these students receive.

Teacher participants often serve as leaders within the project and its component activities, contributing to administrative as well as curricular decisions. In addition, teachers have themselves initiated innovative project elements, such as the Family Computers Program developed by district elementary teachers.

POSTSECONDARY PARTICIPANTS have responded to the opportunity to work with secondary and elementary schools, to be involved in the various component activities, and to participate fully in the faculty forums. STEP Components such as the Family Math Program and Integrated Mathematics/Science Instruction involve an increasing number of postsecondary faculty in elementary and secondary education. Colleges and universities use videotapes of Santa Ana teachers to demonstrate model lessons in bilingual education to teacher candidates. The Departments of Developmental Biology, Chemistry, Mathematics and Fine Arts at the University of California, Irvine, are involved in a variety of related collaborative projects with the school district. Specific partnership programs like the Family Math program carried out by California State University, Fullerton have had a significant effect on parent involvement in their children's education. Under the direction of UC Irvine's Educational Opportunity Program, a quarterly newsletter in Spanish and English is sent home to parents with information regarding meetings and workshops held for them throughout the school year.

PARTICIPANTS FROM ALL LEVELS have formed unusually strong working relationships which cut across institutional boundaries and draw expertise from other programs into the project. Three examples demonstrate the breadth of this phenomena: (1) Project Santa Ana/Fullerton Elementary Mathematics Project (SAFEMAP), an NSF grant coordinated by California State University, Fullerton and the SAUSD, has been associated with Project STEP through the Family Math program, a mutual initiative of the two projects; (2) The UC Irvine Writing project--a site of the California and National Writing Projects--has drawn upon the expertise of the Santa Ana K-12 teachers to become Teacher/Consultants for the Writing Project, particularly in the area of instructional strategies for the multilingual/multicultural classroom; and (3) At an articulation conference co-sponsored by the UCI Partnership Network, which is comprised of representatives from nineteen educational institutions in greater Orange County, Santa Ana and other K-12 teachers were major presenters to an audience of community college faculty. This conference was hosted at Rancho Santiago College and co-sponsored by the Santa Ana district, Rancho Santiago College, and other institutions involved in this network. The conference is the first in a series of discipline-specific forums that have been developed with the support of Project STEP partners.

PARENTS are becoming more involved in their children's education through partnership programs. Programs currently offered for parents include the Family Math program; parent receptions and workshops on topics related to both parenting and college preparation; comprehensive annual conferences at Rancho Santiago Community College; social activities such as the annual Parents' Picnic; and financial aid and career planning workshops. Each of these programs is aimed at establishing closer working relationships between parents and personnel from the educational institutions to strengthen the design of programs for parents and their children.

Checklist of Important Organizational Features of Partnerships

PARTNER INSTITUTIONS

To what extent:

- ☐ Do the partner institutions display long term commitment?
- ☐ Are the partner institutions committed to shared governance within the project?
- ☐ Are the partner institutions committed to ongoing evaluation?

ADMINISTRATIVE COUNCIL

- ☐ Has an Administrative Council been established?
- ☐ Are the majority of Administrative Council members in stable positions?
- ☐ Has the partnership established a Teacher Advisory Committee?

OBJECTIVES AND IMPLEMENTATION PLAN

- ☐ Is there coequal participation in the development of component objectives and activities?
- ☐ Do the component objectives have sufficient scope to address the goals of all participant institutions?
- ☐ Has a focused implementation plan been developed which includes mechanisms for communication and on-going evaluation?
- ☐ Have resources been identified to support intersegmental activity?

CHAPTER 2

Defining the Initial Objectives of the Partnership

Happy marriages are well-known to be rare; just because it lies in the nature of marriage that its chief end is not the present but the coming generation (Arthur Schopenhauer, ***World as Will and Idea,*** 1819).

- *How to identify shared goals*
- *How to integrate complementary goals*
- *How to resolve onflicting goals*
- *How to develop strategies and specific objectives to satisfy collective and institutional partnership goals*

PARTNERS in educational collaboratives, as in personal relationships, come together with different backgrounds, values and goals. The successful collaboratives, which establish long-term commitment and active involvement, are, as in personal relationships, those which can balance the needs and interests of all the partners involved, despite inherent differences.

In forming an educational collaborative, a partnership must begin a process of self-examination and a dialogue with other institutional partners. A series of questions will be helpful in establishing the project's principles, strategies and goals.

How can the partnership identify shared goals?

The underlying principle of partnership objectives is that they must align with the long-range plans of each participating institution. Otherwise, the partnership will be seen as peripheral to the core practices of the district and postsecondary institutions or worse, an intrusion or an impediment rather than a valuable resource.

Project STEP and its participant institutions began with a shared overall educational goal. Originating within the UC Irvine Educational Opportunity Program, Project STEP was designed to improve the academic preparation of all students and, in particular, minority youth, for success in higher education. "Minority" students currently comprise 92% of the student population of Santa Ana Unified School District. The school district serves the greatest proportion of minority students in any area of California. The Santa Ana District has the greatest identified need in the county and state for assistance to meet the needs of its rapidly growing Limited English Proficient (LEP) students. Project STEP's overall mission to enhance the educational opportunities of minority students brings to the school district's primary purpose a vast resource of proven ideas and strategies and to the postsecondary institutions a challenging agenda of research, development, and practitioner training.

How can the partnership integrate complementary goals?

Even when overall goals are in concert, more specific articulation of project objectives is necessary to ensure the commitment of a school district and postsecondary institutions to a partnership project. An example of complementary institutional objectives found among STEP participants is provided below. As STEP entered into the second phase of its history--as "A Partnership for the Advancement of Learning"--discussions were held during STEP Administrative Council meetings for the purpose of identifying the needs of each of the partner institutions and arriving at a mutual agenda.

Needs expressed on the part of the **Santa Ana Unified School District** included the following:

- The need to revise the science and mathematics curriculum in light of the new State ***Model Curriculum Standards;*** and ***Curriculum Frameworks;***

- The need for greater attention to instructional methods in mathematics and science;

- The need for earlier intervention involving parents at key transition points in their children's education to increase the number of minority students who are able to persist into advanced coursework in mathematics and science;

- The need for future teachers in mathematics and science, particularly those from minority groups.

The **postsecondary partners** (Chapman College,* CSU Fullerton, Rancho Santiago Community College, UC Irvine), agreed on the following priorities:

- The need to improve the academic preparation of underrepresented minority students.

- The need to improve curricular continuity between the secondary and postsecondary sectors, particularly in the areas of mathematics and science.

- The need to enhance the preparedness of future teachers in school districts with a significant number of underrepresented minorities and Limited English Proficient students.

A set of five goals were developed as **Project STEP's response** to these needs. The first two goals focused attention on the curricular needs of both the partner school district and the postsecondary institutions, and the balance were committed to the development of a comprehensive partnership model for institutionalization and dissemination:

- Improved academic preparation for all students, particularly of underrepresented minorities in mathematics and science;

---

* Chapman College is the one institution within the Project STEP partnership which is no longer a participant.

- Development of future teachers in mathematics and science, especially those drawn from under-represented minority groups;

- Development of a comprehensive model of educational reform which addresses the areas of curriculum review, staff development and student academic preparation;

- Institutionalization of the model and its components through the establishment of a permanent inter-segmental partnership;

- Dissemination of the program, its components, and the partnership model to the K-12 and post-secondary education communities.

The last three goals incorporate the belief that the underlying philosophy and methodological approach of Project STEP can be applied successfully to any intersegmental partnership if the same collaborative principles are practiced.

How can the partnership resolve conflicting goals?

Too often collaboratives between postsecondary and K-12 institutions fail because of a lack of equal participation in the selection of goals and strategies for achieving them. The dominance of the postsecondary partner or the failure to engage important people not only in executive positions but at the site level (site administrators, teachers, parents and students) can bring about the early demise of a partnership project.

Conflicting goals may emerge in early discussions among partnership members or in the early stages of implementation. Sometimes apparent discrepancies are based on a lack of communication; sometimes the lack of communication itself is based on failure to involve appropriate individuals in the decision-making process. Perhaps more often, the discrepancies can only be explained by acknowledging that certain "hierarchical" and "turf" assumptions are deeply ingrained, and while not deliberate, they are especially destructive in the delicate process of establishing new working relationships.

Project STEP began part of its involvement with the Santa Ana Unified School District under the mistaken understanding that its curricular emphasis should be improving reading skills. This need corresponded neatly with the areas of expertise of several individuals from the postsecondary level who were involved in planning the first initiatives. However, the district's curricular focus had shifted from reading to mathematics. The problems that arose from this conflict in priorities was eventually resolved and Project STEP channelled necessary resources to support a new district initiative in mathematics curriculum development.

Another and more serious tension that STEP experienced in its first phase was that created by the tendency of the postsecondary partners to think traditionally in terms of a "service" model--STEP proceeded by introducing two convenient "inservice" courses for the teachers of the Santa Ana district, for which graduate level units or salary increment points could be earned. Undoubtedly these courses in fact covered valuable new instructional strategies in "Critical Thinking" applied to reading and to writing, and did serve the purpose of familiarizing a large number of the district teachers with practical lesson plans they could use in the classroom. However, the relationship of university professor to K-12 teacher perpetuated in some of these seminars was a direct contradiction of the district's vision to build teachers' confidence and skills as educational leaders.

Luckily, by means of honest discussion and the positive relationships developed in the partnership, these issues were pointed out and amended. During the next two years of the project, "inservice" courses were co-coordinated by district and postsecondary faculty and redesigned to support the district's staff development plan: teachers who participated developed demonstration lesson plans based on their research which were presented to their colleagues in STEP Faculty Forums.

Some goals may be so conflictual that they will seriously impede a partnership from developing. For example, a school district or postsecondary institution may adhere strongly to a hierarchical approach to educational management. Such an institution would not be receptive to Project STEP's collaborative approach. Whatever the degree of conflict that may emerge, it is important that early discussions between partnership members identify and clarify goals and values, and establish working collaborative principles accordingly.

How can the partnership develop the specific strategies and objectives which will satisfy its collective and institutional goals?

From the outset, the STEP Administrative Council has been committed to shared governance, open communication, and coequal participation as guiding principles. External evaluations of Project STEP have emphasized that a major factor in the project's success has been its truly participatory nature, and have pointed to "the almost universal commitment to action" and the collegial relationship between all levels of participants that encourages a steady flow of information and ideas.

These working collaborative principles have been fundamental to Project STEP's ability to empower and engage institutions and individuals in all sectors of the partnership. Moreover, Project STEP has clearly demonstrated adherence to these principles. They are expressed in partnership activities, reports and dissemination. They are further actualized in the partnership governance structure and in the development of project components. As stated by one external evaluator:

> Through this collaborative approach, the curriculum is strengthened, teachers develop collegial relationships with their postsecondary peers, personnel from all of the institutions experience more opportunities for professional development, and increased numbers of students enroll in college preparatory classes and pursue postsecondary education (Van de Water 1989).

These accomplishments, which represent major milestones for Project STEP, are the results of a set of component strategies that translated the general goals of STEP into discrete action agendas: general goals were reduced to achievable objectives. Perhaps a useful summary of the set of processes/actions utilized by Project STEP to get started is the following:

- Establish working collaborative principles
- Derive a comprehensive set of component objectives from general goals
- Assign responsibility for component objectives to a partner institution
- Develop intersegmental teams/task forces to develop specific component objectives
- Devise component program implementation strategies and measurable objectives
- Report periodically to Administrative Council on implementation

During the implementation phase of the 1987-1990 plan, each STEP partner institution assumed coordinating responsibility for at least one of the ten components. This is important in relation to the underlying principles of genuine partnerships and is explained in greater detail in Chapter Five, *Achieving Meaningful Involvement of All Constituency Groups.* Committees, task forces and other forms of intersegmental teams were devised to work under the leadership of a particular institution to design specific component objectives, identify resource needs, and develop implementation strategies including personnel responsibilities, measurable objectives and timelines. The resulting "STEP Components" were composed of an array of dynamic, innovative strategies utilizing the unique resources of the participant institutions. Reports by the STEP Component coordinators on the progress of implementation have been provided regularly to the STEP Administrative Council. Continued open communication about goals and implementation plans is a key factor in partnership cohesion and stability, and will be discussed in Chapter 8, *Communicating for Partnership Cohesion and Dissemination.*

PROJECT COMPONENT DESCRIPTIONS

MATHEMATICS AND SCIENCE ACADEMIC PREPARATION

1. Teams of Santa Ana Unified School District teachers have worked with postsecondary faculty on INTEGRATING MATHEMATICS/ SCIENCE INSTRUCTION. These instructional teams have revised curricular units to incorporate the benefits of interdisciplinary team teaching and intersegmental perspectives in these interdependent disciplines. (COMPONENT #l)

2. FACULTY FORUMS IN MATHEMATICS AND SCIENCE have been initiated to discuss such issues as major curricular changes and student assessment practices. Smaller task force groups initiated under this component have been responsible for development of teacher resource guides in science and design of new assessment practices in mathematics.(COMPONENT #2)

3. A FAMILY MATHEMATICS PROGRAM, developed by the Lawrence Hall of Science at U.C. Berkeley, has been implemented to involve parents and their children in innovative and enjoyable family-based strategies for learning mathematics in their homes. (COMPONENT #3)

FUTURE TEACHER RECRUITMENT

4. A TASK FORCE ON FUTURE TEACHERS has designed strategies to encourage students to consider teaching as a career. (COMPONENT #4)

5. SCHOOL-SITE STUDENT ACADEMIC ADVANCEMENT PROGRAMS have been undertaken to enhance educational aspirations among minority students. (COMPONENT #5)

6. CAREER INTEREST SEMINARS, as well as SKILLS ASSESSMENT PROGRAMS, have been integrated into academic planning sessions for students and their parents. A system for follow-up monitoring of student progress through the SAUSD and into postsecondary educational institutions has been developed. (COMPONENT #6)

7. COOPERATIVE LEARNING LABS have been established which offer tutorial support provided by high school students for courses in mathematics and sciences within the Santa Ana high schools. A pilot at the middle/junior high school level, which utilizes university and community college students as tutors, has been especially effective in fostering interest in the teaching profession. The Cooperative Learning Laboratories have enabled underepresented students currently at partnership high schools, colleges and universities to participate in learning activities while at the same time assisting their peers' development of cognitive skills. (COMPONENT #7)

FACULTY FORUMS/PROFESSIONAL DEVELOPMENT

8. CRITICAL THINKING IN THE LANGUAGE ARTS has been encouraged through the development of a comprehensive teacher resource guide. (COMPONENT #8)

9. FACULTY FORUMS have served as a setting for teachers to learn from each other. Instructors from K-12 schools and postsecondary institutions have shared pedagogical and research ideas and concerns related to specific disciplines and to the enhancement of learning and educational programs for underrepresented students. (COMPONENT #9)

10. INSTRUCTIONAL GUIDANCE CURRICULUM materials have been developed in an articulated program spanning grades six through twelve. (COMPONENT #10)

Evaluation activities have been designed to assist in the implementation and monitoring of each project component. These activities are discussed in Chapter 7, *Evaluating Partnerships.*

A Step-by-Step Approach to the Achievement of Initial Objectives

1. Assess and prioritize the immediate needs of the school district partner in terms of:
- ❑ curriculum development
- ❑ student support services
- ❑ teacher preparation/ enrichment
- ❑ funding initiatives

2. Assess and prioritize the immediate needs of the postsecondary partners in terms of:
- ❑ preparation of incoming students
- ❑ future teacher preparation
- ❑ research interests
- ❑ curriculum development

3. Confirm the long-term goals of the school district.

4. Confirm the long-term goals of the postsecondary partners.

5. Establish a limited set of partnership goals which incorporate both secondary and postsecondary goals.

6. Define working collaborative principles.

7. Derive a set of project component objectives from general goals.

8. Establish a time-line for accomplishment of component objectives.

9. Assign responsibility for specific project components to each partner institution.

10. Each partner institution selects task force committee to develop specific component objectives and resource needs.

11. Task forces design program implementation strategies and measurable objectives in each component.

12. Progress reports on component objectives/ activities are shared with the administrative council for review and dissemination among intersegmental partners.

E V A L U A T I O N: Ongoing and differentiated.

CHAPTER 3

Establishing the Administrative Council: An Intersegmental Core Team

Who cannot what he will, let him will what he can.

(Leonardo da Vinci, quoted by Jose Ortega Y Gasset in ***Mission of the University*** 1944).

- *What are the important characteristics of the Administrative Council--an intersegmental core team?*
- *Who should be on the Administrative Council?*
- *What is the function of an Administrative Council purpose statement?*
- *What types of activities constitute an Administrative Council meeting?*
- *What are the important subcommittees?*
- *A checklist of key individuals and a checklist of administrative committees*

BASED on his experience with the State University of New York (SUNY) Purchase, Westchester School Partnership, Professor Gross offers this strong admonition to potential partnership leaders:

> The steering committee is the critical group in a partnership, and its structure must be carefully considered, particularly if the enterprise is to grow beyond its founding members (Gross 1988, 37).

What are the important characteristics of an Administrative Council?

In the governance study on school-college collaboratives sponsored by the College Board which included observations on Project STEP, Gordon B. Van de Water commented on the essential contribution of Project STEP's Administrative Council to the partnership:

> The most critical factor (in the success of Project STEP) . . . is the almost universal commitment to action . . . Participants . . . know the local conditions, they see the future, and they agree that they want to do something. This pervasive attitude . . . seems to be rippling out to include an ever-increasing circle of teachers, parents, and administrators within the school district and professors and administrators at the four colleges and universities in the area (Van de Water 1989).

Second, he referred to the "extensive local, state and national connections project leaders tap to support STEP activities" (Van de Water 1989, 20). Clearly, for Van de Water, the Administrative Council members have been characterized by a shared commitment to implementation of project goals and by independent professional expertise and influence. Additionally, Project STEP's leaders have been equally representative of all the partner institutions. Faculty and administrators from one segment or one institution have not dominated the council, either in numbers or in attitude.

A key member of any partnership steering committee is the executive director. Project STEP currently has two executive co-directors: The Santa Ana Unified School District Superintendent Dr. Rudy Castruita, and the original university-based executive director, UC Irvine's Assistant Vice Chancellor of Student Affirmative Action, Manuel Gomez.

In ***Partners in Education: How Colleges Can Work with Schools to Improve Teaching and Learning,*** Gross describes in some detail the characteristics of an effective partnership executive director. According to Gross, the executive director (a) is usually drawn from the college that developed the partnership project, (b) should be full-time, in order to maintain total control of all administrative details, and (c) must possess the following administrative traits: sensitivity to people at all levels of responsibility, the ability to plan effectively as he or she shapes an academic vision and matches expectations to reality, and a self-starting style (Gross 1988, 40). Goodlad also perceives the role of executive director to be crucial. He refers to Lieberman's account of partnership leaders as "idea champions" and he goes on to describe several characteristics that successful executive directors share:

> There is no question that persistence, identified by Sarason as an important trait, is crucial. Beyond this, it appears that ability to relate in an open, honest way (to be "authentic" as the concept often is described) to a wide range of groups and individuals, and to listen, are important characteristics. One must be able to move readily back and forth between the culture of the school and the culture of the university, to have an understanding and an appreciation of the values of both, and to be perceived as contemptuous of neither . . . Perhaps more important than the promulgation of ideas may be the ability to draw ideas from others and move them into a common agenda and strategies for action. The ability to question and even challenge others without being threatening, to supply information and resources at critical junctures, and to foster the use of relevant data in all inquiry appears to be a productive, though perhaps rare, trait (Goodlad 1988, 220).

Who Should Be on the Administrative Council?

The STEP Administrative Council is composed of key policy makers from each of the four participating institutions. Although exact representation may vary with each partnership, the following individuals should be considered for membership in the Administrative Councils of other collaboratives:

From the K-12 School District:

- The District Superintendent
- The Director of Secondary Curriculum
- The Director of Elementary Curriculum
- The Director of Staff Development
- The Director of Research, Testing and Evaluation
- Selected Elementary and Secondary School Principals

- Teacher Association Representative
- District Mentor Teacher(s) in Targeted Disciplines
- School Site Facilitator(s) for Partnership Initiatives
- The Public Information Officer

Note: A Project Director and Associate Director should be appointed from the K-12 level.

From the Postsecondary Institutions:

- Vice Chancellor or Assistant Vice Chancellor of Academic Affairs
- Vice Chancellor or Assistant Vice Chancellor of Student Affairs
- Director of Student Outreach Services
- Director or Assistant Director of Education Department
- Faculty in targeted disciplines (e.g., Mathematics, Science, English)
- Other Key Resource Persons (e.g.,Deans of Letters and Science; Director of Community College Learning Center, etc.)

Note: A Project Director and Project Associate Director should be appointed from the postsecondary level.

Student, Parent and Business/Industry Representation:

- A Student Representative
- A Representative for Parents
- A Business Partner

Note: The STEP Project is expanding its membership to include these individuals.

Chief Executive Officers of the Administrative Council:

- Chancellors and Presidents of each participating institution

Note: The C.E.O.'s do not normally participate in Council meetings. They are kept informed of all proceedings and attend on special occasions and when Council is hosted.

What is the Function of the Administrative Council's Purpose Statement?

The Administrative Council's purpose statement is a very important document. It establishes the responsibilities of the council and causes the leadership to articulate the values and principles of the partnership as a whole.

The Purpose Statement of the STEP Administrative Council is reproduced completely at the end of this chapter. The key objectives it sets for the council include the following:

- To provide the leadership, planning and coordination necessary to achieve the long-range goals of Project STEP and to constantly reassess these goals to assure that they are both ambitious and realistic;

- To serve the needs of the individual institutions which council members represent but to be always aware of the larger context and goals related to improving the educational futures of the students whom they serve;

- To oversee established activities of the project and to initiate new ones, with the consistent support of appropriate evaluation techniques;

- To make certain that the administrations of the partner institutions are familiar with the council's activities and in agreement with its goals;

- To be responsible for written statements of purpose and of plans:

There should be annual planning statements concerning anticipated developments for that year. These should bear a clear relationship to a long-term planning statement. Such statements can be expected to lead to the definition of a model which will allow flexibility within concrete plans, and which may eventually be helpful to other communities;

- To provide a general structure for the ongoing STEP program; to develop, enhance and broaden that program; to discover what problems or issues need attention; to seek solutions; and to give voice to the purposes and activities which it will guide. The Council's specific duties will emerge from these major aims.

What Types of Activities Constitute an Administrative Council Meeting?

The STEP Administrative Council members are appointed to three-year terms by the chief executive officers of each participating institution. The Council, which meets a minimum of four times each year, elects a Chair and one Vice Chair. A practice of rotating meeting sites to be hosted by each partner institution permits the C.E.O. an opportunity to directly participate in the deliberations of the Council.

A typical Administrative Council meeting might include the following activities:

Directors' Reports

- Overview of recent activities of the partnership;
- Identification of goals and efforts warranting particular emphasis in the near future;
- Calendar reminders--including project activities, evaluation, dissemination and dates.

Overview of Current Partnership Initiatives
- Reports of project components;
- Commitments of partnership institutions;
- Resource and dissemination opportunities.

Updates from Subcommittees
- Description of specific component activities;
- Overview(s) by subcommittee representatives.

STEP Facilitators' Reports
- Reports by representatives from specific school sites and postsecondary institutions concerning individual programs;
- Descriptions of particular student needs that merit attention.

Report from the Teacher Advisory Committee
- Reactions of teachers to particular partnership programs;
- Requests for specific Faculty Forums and professional development opportunities.

Data Management Committee Reports
- Updates on evaluation results, including findings concerning designated programs;
- Requests for attention to or assistance on specific data collection and/or evaluation and reporting needs.

Next Steps: Planning Discussion
- Identification of new directions, initiatives, task force development;
- Decisions regarding potential policy directions;
- Decisions regarding resource priorities and planning.

It is important to note here that, as well as sharing ideas, information and concerns, the Administrative Council provides an opportunity for the leadership to publicly discuss and recognize the accomplishments of specific institutions, task forces, and individuals. The underlying interpersonal dynamics are discussed in greater depth in Chapter Eight, *Communicating for Partnership Cohesion and Dissemination,* but it can be seen from this example of an

Administrative Council agenda that many different members of the partnership are given the opportunity to address the group and serve as significant team players. It is also important to note that accurate and detailed minutes must be kept of all Administrative Council meetings for dissemination within the partnership and for possible evaluation purposes.

What are the Important Subcommittees?

Not all the committees were created at the beginning of the STEP project. Some have emerged to include a greater number of core people involved in administrative decision-making. Greater influence on and participation in the decision-making process brings greater commitment and resources from the various members from each partnership institution.

Of the STEP Council Subcommittees, the Data Management/Evaluation Committee and the Teacher Advisory Committee are standing committees, with a formalized relationship to the Administrative Council. Additional subcommittee functions have been variously assigned to permanent task forces or ad hoc committees, a full list of which includes the following:

1. *Data Management and Evaluation Committee*
    - *Responsible for* internal evaluation needs and for assisting to fulfill funding agency reporting requirements.
    - *Involves* key evaluation and data management specialists from partner institutions in project monitoring and assessment.

2. *Teacher Advisory Committee*
    - *Responsible* for articulating K-12 faculty interests and needs with the development of project component and evaluation tasks.
    - *Involves* school district faculty in assessment of school district needs and implementation strategies.

3. ***Faculty Forum/Professional Development***
   - *Responsible for* intersegmental and programmatic conference design and implementation in such disciplinary areas as the following: mathematics; science; language arts (including bilingual and English as a second language initiatives); guidance and student support; future teacher recruitment and support.
   - *Involves* lead staff and faculty in key disciplines from partner institutions.

4. ***Resource Planning***
   - *Responsible for* external and internal budget support.
   - *Involves* key program and budget staff (including grant writers) from the participating institutions.

5. ***Student Activities Coordination***
   - *Responsible for* student academic advancement programs and future teachers initiatives at each school site, complemented by college university outreach support.
   - *Involves* school site principals and administration, key people from student affairs, student support programs, career guidance, and staff designated to involve parents in school programs.

6. ***Dissemination***
   - *Responsible for* internal and external dissemination via conference representation, professional articles, media and publicity, and related dissemination forums.
   - *Involves* key program staff and public information officers and media resource persons.

Purpose Statement: Project STEP Administrative Council

Purpose of the Council

The Council will provide the leadership, planning, and coordination necessary to achieve the long-range goals of the STEP project. It has responsibility to assure that these goals are constantly renewed and perceived as both ambitious and realistic. Its context is the educational systems in which its participants function, but its final concern is with the students whose futures are shaped, in part, by the nature and quality of the education available to them. The Council exists on the assumption that this education can be improved.

The Council will oversee all proposed major activities of the project, and will consider itself responsible also for the initiation of concepts and activities. In addition, it will construct some suitable means of evaluating STEP activities and its own activities periodically.

Since the STEP project is a collaborative effort involving a number of institutions, an important obligation of the Council will be to make certain that the administrations of those institutions are familiar with its activities and in agreement with its goals.

All of these purposes require clarity about both short- and long-term goals, intentions, and plans for action. For this reason the Council will be responsible for the development of written statements of purpose and of plans. There should be annual planning statements concerning anticipated developments for that year. These should bear a clear relationship to a long-term planning statement. Such statements can be expected to lead to the definition of a model which will allow flexibility with concrete plan, and which may eventually be helpful to other communities.

In summary, the Council is intended to provide a structure for the ongoing STEP program; to develop, enhance, and broaden that program; to discover what problems or issues need attention; to seek solutions; and to give voice to the purposes and activities which it will guide. The Council's specific duties will emerge from these major aims.

Appointment to the Council

Council members are appointed by the chief executive officers of their institutions. In order to assure continuity, Council members will normally be appointed for three-year terms. The Council will decide whether these terms should be renewable and whether action is necessary to bring new members into the Council. Ex-officio members as appropriate shall be appointed by the Council.

Officers

Officers will serve a minimum of one year. A Chair will be elected by the Council. The Chair will be responsible for establishing specific procedures and for preparing the agendas for the meetings. In addition, two Vice Chairs will be elected. One will assist the Chair and will serve in his or her place when necessary. The other will be responsible for communications. Secretarial services will be provided by the Chair's institution.

Frequency of Meetings

The Council will meet formally at least four times a year. However, it will be prepared to meet whenever necessary. The Council may wish to appoint a subcommittee to deal with matters requiring frequent meetings.

Duration of Council

The Council should continue to exist until it is no longer needed.

A Checklist of Key Individuals for an Administrative Council

Does the Administrative Council include the following key people?

From the school district:

- ❑ District Superintendent?
- ❑ Associate and Assistant Superintendents?
- ❑ Project Director and Associate Director?
- ❑ Director of Secondary Curriculum?
- ❑ Director of Elementary Curriculum?
- ❑ Director of Staff Development?
- ❑ Director of Research, Testing and Evaluation?
- ❑ Principals of participating schools?
- ❑ Teacher Association Representative?
- ❑ District Mentor Teacher in targeted disciplines?
- ❑ School Site Facilitators for partnership initiatives?
- ❑ Public Information Officer?

From the postsecondary partner institutions:

- ❑ Chancellors/Presidents?
- ❑ Project Director and Associate Director?
- ❑ Vice Chancellor or Assistant Vice Chancellor of Academic Affairs?
- ❑ Vice Chancellor or Assistant Vice Chancellor of Student Affairs?
- ❑ Director of Student Outreach Services?
- ❑ Director or Assistant Director of Teacher Education Department?
- ❑ Faculty in targeted disciplines (e.g., Mathematics, Science, English)
- ❑ Other Key Resource Persons?

- ❑ Are the Chief Executive Officers of each partner institution committed to the partnership and kept informed of the Administrative Council deliberations?

  Will the Administrative Council include:
  - ❑ A student representative?
  - ❑ A parent representative?
  - ❑ A business partner?

- ❑ Is someone assigned to record and disseminate minutes of Administrative Council Meetings?

A Checklist of Administrative Committees

- ❑ An Administrative Council which includes representation by each key partnership subgroup
- ❑ A Data Management/Evaluation Committee
- ❑ A Teacher Advisory Committee
- ❑ Resource Planning Committee
- ❑ Project Component Committees
- ❑ Student Activities Committee
- ❑ Dissemination Committee

CHAPTER 4

Identifying and Securing Fiscal and Human Resources

> *A key factor in local alliances, unsurprisingly, is money. And a central issue in the most successful programs is how to free them from their extraordinary degree of dependence on the philanthropic foundations. Foundations have the major force in launching the alliances. They cannot be expected to be the primary agent that keeps them going* (Atkin and Atkin 1989, 145).

How to Utilize Resources:

- *At the postsecondary Level*
- *At the school district level*
- *From external funding agencies*

PARTNERSHIPS must not think too narrowly about the whole subject of resources. It is extremely important to actively seek out major external sources, for example, but the very concept of a partnership implies reciprocity of resources within the partnership itself. These internal resources, both human and financial, will exist before and after various grants; they can facilitate enormously the institutionalization of a partnership and they can be channelled more precisely to fit partnership needs.

Project STEP has been fortunate to receive support from major funding sources, including California Academic Partnership Program, the Carnegie Corporation of New York, and the College Board's Educational EQuality Project. It has also made full use of the human and financial resources available through the four partnership institutions.

Gordon B. Van de Water emphasizes both the action orientation and the extensive local, state and national connections project leaders have brought to STEP Administrative Council meetings: "They shared this information easily, almost casually, yet it was the kind of information that would open doors to needed expertise and fiscal resources" (Van de Water 1989). His reference to the "almost universal commitment to action" of participants indicates the type of "grass-roots" support that enables partnerships to prosper and survive.

How to Utilize Resources at the Postsecondary Level

Postsecondary Administrators

Chief Executive Officers must be kept closely informed of partnership activities through minutes from Administrative Council meetings, personal briefings and the like. Their demonstration of commitment to the project brings access to a wide range of resources, fiscal and human. One of the unique aspects of the STEP partnership has been the extremely strong commitment of the C.E.O.s of the participating postsecondary institutions. As well as creating a climate of personal support within their institutions, several of the leaders have committed specific funding: Since 1987, for example, the President of California State University, Fullerton, has contributed $5,000 yearly to the partnership budget, and the Chancellor of Rancho Santiago Community College has supported the tutorial component of Project STEP by direct payment of peer tutor salaries totaling over $5,000 each year.

Postsecondary administrators responsible for academic affairs, campus outreach, relations with secondary schools, and campus student support areas can provide valuable experience, as well as access to human and fiscal resources. From their perspective, a partnership such as STEP can provide a problem-solving mechanism that assists them in establishing better communication and coordination between the K-12 and postsecondary level. Project STEP has involved a wide range of postsecondary administrators whose functions it can assist:

- Vice-Chancellors of Student Services and Academic Affairs;
- Directors of Student Academic Services and University Outreach Programs;
- Coordinators of Student Affirmative Action Programs;
- Directors of Teacher Education Programs;

- Directors of Learning Resource Centers;
- Directors of Programs Dealing with Relations with Schools and Colleges; and
- Directors of English as a Second Language Programs.

Administrators' commitment to the project will be enhanced if their responsibilities are facilitated by the success of the project. For example, Directors of Educational Opportunity Programs are responsible for the recruitment and retention of underrepresented students; they will be supportive of program components that will complement their role in this area. One EOP Director in Project STEP took on the initial leadership role in sponsoring the first STEP partnership-wide counselors conference, which developed collaborative instructional guidance component activities. Another administers the Parents in Partnership Program, which coordinates all parent informational meetings and conferences. Their roles in Project STEP have been directly and easily connected to their other institutional responsibilities and functions.

In fact, the professional and administrative support staff at each of the partner institutions provide a major resource of STEP. Each year since 1987 a total of over three hundred faculty, administrators, staff, and counselors have committed a portion of their work week to collaborative initiatives under various STEP components that have become "the way of doing business" among the partner institutions. The skills and talents of dedicated administrative staff assistants to help provide the communications support necessary for coordination of these STEP programs represent a significant in-kind institutional contribution to the success of partnership efforts. Another prominent example of the type of professionals that any partnership will rely on and must recruit is the data management/evaluation staff of each institution, whose responsibilities are manifold.

Postsecondary Faculty

Key postsecondary faculty must be recruited for leadership roles within project components. Faculty at the postsecondary level may join partnerships for a variety of reasons, which are not necessarily dependent on their institutional affiliation. Some perceive their participation to be a public service in preparing students for college and to the community at-large. Other faculty have a history of developing freshman year programs for the benefit of incoming students, and their contribution may be more oriented towards articulation between secondary and postsecondary instruction. A third group of faculty view participation in an academic partnership as having enormous benefits to both their research and teaching. This last group is usually drawn from the behavioral and social sciences and the field of education.

Historically, most academic partnerships have been associated with postsecondary schools of education. Project STEP has sought, successfully, to recruit faculty and administrators campuswide. This emphasis on broad campus involvement in the collaboration was established from its inception. In 1983, when Project STEP was first launched as an independent partnership, the Vice Chancellor of UC Irvine was Dr. William Lillyman. He was later asked how, under his direction, Project STEP managed to bring together a great variety of groups, persons, and projects--including Student Affirmative Action, the Office of Teacher Education, the UCI Writing Project, the campus' Summer Science Project, and faculty members from a number of academic departments. Usually these university-based groups would be quite separated, either because of different administrative structures or because of differences in orientation or aim. His answer regarding the unusual, multi-faceted nature of the campus involvement was:

> [Thus,] my answer to the question . . . is the following:
>
> 1. During the past three years, a number of people worked hard to define the problems and to imagine ways in which we might address them within the limitations of the funding available to us.
>
> 2. Structural and administrative changes were made in light of those problems and in order to make the best use of the resources we had.
>
> 3. The forces driving these actions were part of the forces that have caused the campus to seek useful relationships among its organizations. Efforts to improve the schools or provide the best possible

> support services for enrolled students cannot be seen in isolation.
>
> 4. UCI is fortunate in having faculty members from the various disciplines who are genuinely interested in improving the education of prospective students. The mechanisms we have devised and their relationship to each other would not be effective without the participation of our faculty.
>
> I wish to say, finally, that UCI fully recognizes the importance of working to improve the curriculum in the public schools; of working with school administrators; and eventually of working with School Boards. At the same time, UCI knows that the teacher in the classroom is the key to significant change (Lillyman 1983).

Project STEP has continued to engage the commitment of postsecondary faculty from a variety of academic disciplines, units and projects. Faculty from Mathematics, Science and Education Departments in conjunction with K-12 colleagues have developed interdisciplinary teaching, critical thinking/writing and problem-solving curriculum materials. Intersegmental task forces have also undertaken several major externally funded grants to carry out and systematically examine innovative technology-based instructional strategies in such areas as mathematics and science education.

Often an added benefit of involvement with a statewide college or university system can be contact with expert faculty at a number of other institutions. Project STEP has been fortunate to utilize the talents of several professors from a variety of campuses and to tap into programs and projects at several campuses which complement STEP's activities. CSU Fullerton's adaptation for the STEP Project of the Family Math program, developed by the Lawrence Hall of Science at U.C. Berkeley, is an example of this type of interface with other campuses within a university system. A number of academic alliances have also been formed among faculty at local community colleges, which have resulted in similar benefits of shared expertise.

Postsecondary Resources

Existing postsecondary resources may serve an extremely useful purpose for achieving the goals of a partnership. Initiatives developed independently by various academic departments will greatly benefit the partnership, especially when associated with or coordinated through the Administrative Council. Illustrations of such coordination within Project STEP have been the following:

- ***UCI Summer Science and Mathematics Institute***--Many of the activities and strategies described within the Mathematics/Science Components originated from K-12 and postsecondary faculty involvement in these programs.

- ***RSC Science Exchange Program***--This collaborative initiative between Rancho Santiago College and Santa Ana district faculty drew upon the considerable thirst that elementary students have for science education. High school students coached by their teachers shared their science projects with their younger peers at the elementary level. These demonstrations were videotaped and shown as well to the proud parents of these potential future scientists.

- ***UCI Writing Project***--The instructional strategies of the UCI Writing Project have been implemented in many English classes within the district.

- ***CSU Fullerton Project Catalyst***--With a focus in Geology, this project involves K-12 teachers in development of materials, content mastery, and informative field trip programs.

- ***UCI/California Mathematics and Science Teacher Project***--These projects have selected talented K-12 teachers for development of materials for implementation of the California Mathematics and

Science Frameworks and for training in effective strategies of problem presentation. Participants have become knowledgeable about a broad range of current issues in mathematics and science education, including the need to increase the leadership role of women and minorities and approaches for improving the success of underrepresented minority students in these fields.

Student academic support programs already in existence may coordinate their services with project components and contribute to the accomplishment of the partnership goals.

In Project STEP, for example:

- ***The Rancho Santiago Community College Learning Center***--The Director of the Learning Center, with the encouragement of the College Chancellor, utilizes Learning Center facilities and personnel to train peer tutors for the cooperative learning laboratory component of Project STEP.

- ***The UC Irvine Educational Opportunity Program/Student Affirmative Action Outreach Office (EOP/SAA)***--This program, which initiated Project STEP, contributes the support of a variety of its services such as the Junior High and Senior High Partnership Programs and the Parents in Partnership Program. Junior High Partnership officers, trained by representatives of the American College Testing program (ACT), provide feedback and information to the students in STEP who have participated in the ACT Career Planning Program and to their parents in evening workshops. In addition, a joint committee of UCI EOP/SAA staff and Santa Ana Unified School District counselors developed lesson plans on educational planning and goal-setting for the STEP Instructional Guidance Component.

- ***UCI's "Artists-in-Training" Program***-- This program, a collaboration between the UC Irvine School of Fine Arts and EOP/SAA, provides performances at high schools for students and parents. This has given families exposure to some of the cultural activities which are part of students' postsecondary opportunities.

How to Utilize Resources at the K-12 Level

K-12 Administrators

The School District Superintendent in his or her role is crucial in providing leadership and commitment of district human and material resources. Most importantly, the Superintendent can contribute vision and presence to the partnership that will motivate many others within the district. Dr. Rudy Castruita, Superintendent of the Santa Ana Unified School District, constantly reaffirms his support of the Project STEP Partnership. Dr. Castruita's support for expanded and future-oriented collaboration is evident in his comments regarding a partnership proposal focused on cooperative initiatives in technology:

> This **Science 2000: Technology-Based Middle School Science Program** incorporates extraordinary efforts to develop a state-of-the-art, technology-based science program for our seventh grade students, which will be aligned with the new California Science Framework. It will empower our instructional staff with the knowledge of the new curriculum, as well as the application of technology to it. Research demonstrates that this application of technology is critical in assisting our English as a Second Language student population, and the results of our combined school district-university efforts will have great value to the educational community nationwide (Castruita 1989).

The Superintendent can also contribute fiscal resources to particular project components, by, for example, endorsing and allocating funds to conduct and enable faculty to attend inservice workshops that are critical vehicles for professional development.

Other key administrators at the district level can contribute both fiscal and human resources to the project, as well. Examples are as follow:

- ***The Directors of Elementary and Secondary Curriculum*** contribute expertise in the areas of both curricular development and guidance and are crucial to institutionalizing the project, linking it directly with district curriculum goals;

- ***The District Director of Research, Evaluation and Testing and the Assistant Superintendent for Staff Development*** contribute specialized expertise and resources in their respective areas;

- ***The District Special Projects/Grants Writer***---She/he can assist in coordinating new initiatives among the partnership institutions and in writing proposals for external funding for the district that are related to project goals.

School site principals and administrators can facilitate staff and student involvement in school site renewal in a broad variety of ways, with partnership project activities and participation not peripheral but an integrated part of the process. Principals are absolutely essential to establishing and maintaining school site enthusiasm for enacting changes in curriculum and professional development programs to support these changes.

In Project STEP, each principal at the high school level has appointed an individual teacher, administrator or counselor to serve as the STEP Facilitator. This individual is responsible for collaborative activities at the school site and for coordination of efforts districtwide through participation on STEP Task Forces such as the Task Force on Student Outreach.

K-12 Faculty

Clearly, the teacher in the classroom is the key to significant change. It has been STEP's experience that K-12 faculty are often excited about sharing methodologies developed for multicultural, multilingual classrooms with faculty from the postsecondary level and with student teacher credential candidates. Mentor teachers and others who are actively involved in curricular reform are able to contribute ideas and experiences from related projects to the partnership.

For example, mathematics instructional leaders who comprised the STEP intersegmental curriculum review committee in 1985-1986 took lead responsibility in conducting a Project STEP faculty forum called "The Mathematics Leadership Dialogue"--which was co-sponsored by the College Board Educational EQuality Project. These committee members, who had all been participants in the UCI Mathematics Institute, conducted discussions among the department chairs and their colleagues from each of the eleven secondary schools in the district to familiarize them with the new Mathematics Framework and address issues of concern regarding the impact of proposed curricular changes.

K-12 Resources

The development of special student college preparatory programs has been fostered through STEP coordination of resources and dissemination of results. By way of example, at Santa Ana High School, students have the opportunity to join a college-bound "PREP" program created by school site staff, who were subsequently appointed as STEP Facilitators. In this program, students share common core classes which allows release of several classrooms into the auditorium for mini-lectures delivered by professors from various campuses and disciplines. "PREP" teachers assist students in such study skills as note-taking and in understanding college level expectations.

During the initial STEP Faculty Forums in the spring of 1983, good ideas and concepts such as this PREP program were described, and since then each of the high schools has focused attention on developing its own unique program of academic support and guidance for college preparatory students. These "prep" programs, which are often joined in collaboration with student outreach programs from the postsecondary level, have come to be known as the Student Academic Advancement Programs nurtured by Project STEP.

Another major example of channeling existing resources to accomplish important objectives is the development of the Santa Ana district Comprehensive Guidance Program, Grades Six through Twelve, which is further discussed in Chapter 6, *Developing a Model for Student Support Services.*

How to Utilize Resources of External Funding Agencies

Partnerships must ensure that participant institutions are fully informed about external funding to support collaborative activities. Support from state and national public and private agencies can not only provide vital fiscal resources; it also presents a wealth of opportunities for dissemination through conferences, reports and handbooks and offers a partnership many opportunities for networking with other collaboratives.

For example, The California Academic Partnership Program (CAPP), a California legislative initiative created in 1985 by the California State Legislature to cultivate university and college intersegmental cooperation with the K-12 sector, provided Project STEP with the means to extend the range and depth of partnership involvement to include more colleges. The Carnegie Corporation of New York has contributed significant support to Project STEP and, as an example, provided the support resulting in this publication. The College Board Educational EQuality Project funded seed monies for the early Project STEP Parent Summer Bridge programs, the Mathematics Leadership Dialogue described above, and a research project on student participation and persistence in mathematics courses. All of these funding agencies have brought Project STEP into contact with other collaborative efforts as well as the most current reform efforts by means of state and national conferences.

Checklist of Key Resource People

Have the following people and programs within the partnership institutions been recruited to support the partnership?

AT THE POSTSECONDARY LEVEL

- ❑ Chief Executive Officers?
- ❑ Key administrators in academic affairs areas?
- ❑ Key administrators in student support areas?
- ❑ Key faculty and staff in targeted disciplines?
- ❑ Key administrators and faculty in targeted relevant teacher education programs?
- ❑ Institutional research and admissions staff

AT THE K-12 LEVEL

- ❑ Superintendent?
- ❑ Key administrators?
  - Deputy/Assistant Superintendents?
  - Directors of Secondary and Elementary Curriculum?
  - Director of Research, Evaluation and Testing?
  - Grant Writer?
  - School Site Principals, Administrators, and Staff?
- ❑ Key K-12 faculty?
  - Faculty who demonstrate interest and commitment to professional development and renewal?
  - Department chairs?
  - Mentor teachers?
  - Counselors?
  - Teacher Association Leader(s)?

CHAPTER 5

Achieving Meaningful Involvement of All Constituency Groups

Successful companies demonstrate a bias for action. By this the authors mean that the companies fostered experimentation and activity. Instead of large groups working for several months on research and development of specific projects, they form teams of small groups who test out ideas fairly quickly (Peters and Waterman 1982).

> *Lessons from partnership research*
>
> *Project STEP's Approach:*
>
> - *Establishing principles and strategies for meaningful involvement*
> - *Developing meaningful involvement opportunities within project components*

IN A BESTSELLER on business management, ***In Search of Excellence: Lessons from America's Best-Run Companies*** (Peters and Waterman 1982), the authors observe that the most innovative and successful companies that they researched demonstrated several key attributes including the following: a bias for action, good listening skills, risk-taking, reliance on the rank and file for ideas, and simple management structures that support "autonomy and creative involvement from as many employees as possible" (Peters and Waterman 1982). These essential attributes of successful business management may be translated into such recommendations as the following for a multi-institutional educational organization--which is the very nature of an academic partnership:

- create small groups which are action-oriented;
- maintain a large degree of communication between all participants;
- establish a clear, strong set of values;
- develop a simple, lean administrative structure;
- foster autonomy and innovation;
- support creative risk-taking.

Lessons from Partnership Research

On the basis of his experience and research, John Goodlad points out the centrality of several strategies in the organization of successful academic partnerships. Three of these strategies are particularly relevant to the development of "meaningful involvement" in partnership initiatives:

> First, he recommends the development of task forces or working parties, each charged with developing plans and strategies for addressing the most critical and most calcified problems of improving schools and the education of educators, and each staffed with appropriate representation of schools, district offices, and universities (and with consultants from outside any given partnership, as appropriate).
>
> Second, he recommends an orderly process within each partnership of endorsing and encouraging all projects and activities undertaken in the partnership so as to assure widespread understanding and a minimum of bureaucratic procedures and control.
>
> Third, he suggests making arrangements for sharing information, ideas, and even resources within and across partnerships, including the sharing of responsibility of advocating the best in educational policy and practice. (Sirotnik, K. and Goodlad, J. 1988).

In effect, Goodlad is making similar recommendations for academic partnerships as Peters and Waterman did for companies. The caveat exists, however, that educators face the added challenge of facilitating the meaningful involvement of participants from significantly different institutions.

Thus, strategies for meaningful involvement in intersegmental partnerships in education which may be derived from Goodlad's work include the following:

- decide on the educational problems to be tackled;
- develop intersegmental task forces or teams to work on specific problems;
- allow the teams or task forces to develop their own strategies;
- reduce bureaucratic procedures and control; and
- share responsibilities, information, ideas within and across partnerships.

Project STEP's Approach

Establishing Principles and Strategies for Meaningful Involvement

The degree of meaningful involvement that outside evaluators often note in Project STEP may be due in part to the extent to which its behaviors as an intersegmental organizational structure reinforce such attributes as those demonstrated by successful businesses and earlier research concerning academic partnerships. Other chapters, in particular Chapter 6, *Developing a Model for Student Support Services,* discuss the extent to which Project STEP has developed a clear sense of its own meaning in terms of values understood and shared by participants. This chapter will focus on the organizational approach to the productive, energetic involvement of the greatest number of partnership participants. Project STEP's core values of collaboration, coequal participation, shared governance and educational reform are clearly reflected in the component strategies and activities.

The basic principles of the STEP approach to creating meaningful involvement can be outlined as follow:

- general goals are divided into specific components;
- leadership of the components is shared among partner institutions;
- component task forces and committees are often intersegmental;
- staff development is usually based on dialogue, demonstration, participation and implementation rather than didactic presentation;
- regardless of their position in the educational hierarchy, participants have the opportunity to take on leadership roles in component activities;
- instruction and staff development are often interdisciplinary to facilitate greater involvement within as well as between institutions;
- whenever possible, linkages are developed with other institutional projects related to the component;
- component activities emphasize strategies designed to make education more meaningful and more engaging for students, their families and educators. For example, teaching strategies focus on problem-solving, interdisciplinary instruction, critical thinking skills and cooperative learning, while support services facilitate parental involvement and cross-age and peer tutoring by students.

The deliberate administrative strategy of promoting coequal participation and collaboration in administration, teaching and learning has proven extremely successful in achieving Project STEP's curricular goals. This strategy has also developed a strong sense of ownership and commitment to the project on the part of its participants, such that they are constantly identifying new approaches and involving additional people and resources to achieve partnership goals.

Developing Involvement Opportunities Within Project Components

In order to illustrate the different ways in which participants are involved in achieving component goals and objectives, each of Project STEP's components will be analyzed according to the following criteria:

- the goal of the component;
- the lead institution responsible for the component;
- the key participants in the component;
- the key activities used to achieve component objectives.

These components are not described in this format for the sake of identical replication by institutions elsewhere, since each partnership will focus on its particular needs and resources. Rather, they are meant to illustrate (1) the comprehensive scope of Project STEP's goals; (2) the principle of shared responsibility between partnership institutions; and (3) the great variety of activities in which educators can engage in order to both contribute to the project and learn from each other.

COMPONENT ONE:

School Site Mathematics/Science Instructional Teams

GOAL:	To develop and demonstrate lesson plans which integrate the teaching of mathematics and science.
LEAD INSTITUTION:	UCI
PARTICIPANTS:	Postsecondary Mathematics and Science Faculty and secondary instructors

ACTIVITIES:

- Committee meetings
- Faculty Forums
- Demonstration Lessons given by Partnership Fellows in Mathematics and Science
- Professional Development sessions held at secondary and postsecondary institutions
- Campus tours for students to stimulate interest in the fields of mathematics and science
- Summer Institutes

COMPONENT TWO:

Intersegmental Mathematics and Science Curriculum Task Force Committees

GOALS:

1. To revise district mathematics curriculum to conform with the new California ***Model Curriculum Standards***

2. To develop a Science Resource Guide

LEAD INSTITUTION: Santa Ana Unified School District

PARTICIPANTS: School District Director of Curriculum and secondary division faculty-- assisted by postsecondary advisors

ACTIVITIES:

- Mathematics Curriculum Committee
- District Curriculum Review Committee
- Science Resource Guide Development Committee
- Intermediate Grades Science Process Skills Development Committee
- Mathematics Concept Workshops

COMPONENT THREE:

Family Math/Science (Kindergarten Through Sixth Grade)

GOAL: To prepare teachers to work with parents and their elementary school children to increase family interest and participation in mathematics and science learning.

LEAD INSTITUTION: California State University, Fullerton

PARTICIPANTS: Postsecondary mathematics and education faculty--working with kindergarten through grade 6 faculty

ACTIVITIES:

- K-12 Faculty inservice programs using the "Family Math" Program and Project EQUALS , both developed by the Lawrence Hall of Science, UC Berkeley

COMPONENT FOUR:

Task Force on Development of Future Teachers in Math/Science

GOAL:	To recruit minority candidates into the teaching profession
LEAD INSTITUTION:	Chapman College, a private four-year college
PARTICIPANTS:	Representatives from each of the participating postsecondary institutions, in particular faculty from Departments of Education, and outreach program administrators--working with school district personnel.
ACTIVITIES:	• Teachers of Tomorrow Clubs at secondary and postsecondary institutions • Partnership Network Subcommittee on Teacher Recruitment • Workshops for Bilingual Aides, including follow-up campus visits to each institution of higher education and individual counseling and assistance • Cooperative Learning Labs for secondary students to participate in cross-age and peer tutoring

COMPONENT FIVE:

School Site Academic Advancement Programs

GOAL:	To design, pilot and evaluate school-based academic advancement programs for minority students
LEAD INSTITUTION:	Santa Ana Unified School District
PARTICIPANTS:	School District site administrators and guidance and instructional Personnel--working with postsecondary outreach coordinators
ACTIVITIES:	• Junior High Partnership • Santa Ana College Prep Program • Valley Academy Program • Saddleback STEP and UCI Partners Club • Future Teachers Club (at school sites) • UCI: *Steps Toward Excellence* Conference • Comprehensive Guidance Program for grades 6-12

COMPONENT SIX:

Student Needs and Interest Assessment/
Career Workshops for the Family

GOALS: To assess student career needs and interests as a fundamental and ongoing part of the District's new Guidance Program and
To familiarize parents with the educational requirements students must fulfill in order to pursue postsecondary education

LEAD INSTITUTION: University of California, Irvine

PARTICIPANTS: School District's Postsecondary Guidance Coordinator and guidance committee--working with postsecondary representatives (Educational Opportunity Program/Student Affirmative Action Outreach Staff)

ACTIVITIES:

- Career Assessment workshops for secondary students
- American College Testing Program and SAT Workshop
- Career Planning Program workshop
- Parent Night
- Student leadership conferences:
    - "Building Leaders for Tomorrow"
    - "Women in Science and Mathematics"
    - "Hispanic Youth Leadership"
    - "Steps Toward Excellence"
- Monitoring minority students' academic progress at the postsecondary level

COMPONENT SEVEN:

Cooperative Learning Labs and Leaders in Mathematics and Science

GOAL:	To raise the level of achievement of minority students in the areas of mathematics and science and to foster interest in teaching through tutorial teaching teams
LEAD INSTITUTION:	Rancho Santiago Community College
PARTICIPANTS:	Postsecondary faculty and students as trainers; college, senior and junior high school tutors working in paired tutoring teams with postsecondary representatives
ACTIVITIES:	• Cooperative Learning Labs

COMPONENT EIGHT:

Critical Thinking in the Language Arts/ Curriculum Review and Implementation

GOALS: To foster critical thinking skills through writing and

To revise the language arts curriculum of the District

LEAD INSTITUTION: Santa Ana Unified School District

PARTICIPANTS: District teachers working with postsecondary faculty and administrators--in particular, representatives from the UCI Writing Project

ACTIVITIES:

- Adapting the UCI Thinking/Writing Project to create demonstration lessons particularly well-suited for the District to foster critical thinking skills through writing
- Providing training involving teacher consultants from the UCI Thinking/Writing Project
- Preparing teacher resource materials, including grades 6-12 curriculum scope and sequence and lesson samples in language arts
- Securing external funding to develop and evaluate language arts curriculum

COMPONENT NINE:

Faculty Forums

GOALS:

To disseminate information regarding central issues in mathematics and science instruction to teachers in the district

To disseminate innovative ways of presenting mathematics and science content

To engage university faculty in school-based inquiry related to enhancement of secondary programs in mathematics and science for underrepresented students

LEAD INSTITUTION: Santa Ana Unified School District

PARTICIPANTS: School District Teacher Advisory Committee, K-12 and postsecondary faculty; external consultants and Project Fellows

ACTIVITIES:

- Presentations by distinguished faculty members from secondary schools in the region and from postsecondary institutions (e.g., Jaime Escalante, mathematics; Dr. Eloy Rodriguez, biology)

- Externally funded research and development undertaken collaboratively by university faculty and school staff to identify effective instructional practices for underrepresented and language minority students (e.g., University of California Presidential Grant for School Improvement--"Developing Conceptual Understanding in Science: Theory and Practice"; University of California Linguistic Minority Project Grant--"Analyzing the Educational Processes and Outcomes Associated with a Bilingual Videodisc-Based Science Program for Hispanic Middle School Students")

- Inservice training including dialogues between K-12 and postsecondary faculty on disciplinary and cross-disciplinary research and pedagogy

COMPONENT TEN:

Instructional and Guidance Curriculum Development and Implementation

GOALS: To develop a district Comprehensive Guidance Program enabling counselors to address the needs of a highly diverse student population and

To help students understand the important linkages between postsecondary education and careers of interest to them

LEAD INSTITUTION: Santa Ana Unified School District

PARTICIPANTS: Santa Ana Unified School District Counseling Staff and Faculty

ACTIVITIES:

- The establishment of a comprehensive program of services to be provided to all students in the secondary schools of the District

- The articulation of guidance services throughout grades 6 through 12 continuum

- The provision of guidance and counseling strategies in a model enabling counselors' skills and expertise to be used in addressing the needs of the District's highly diverse population

- Guidance Service Conferences

A Checklist for Achieving Meaningful and Comprehensive Involvement

- ❑ Have larger goals been broken down into separate initiatives?
- ❑ Has each partner institution taken primary responsibility for one or more specific objectives?
- ❑ Have small task forces been selected to develop and implement strategies to meet component objectives?
- ❑ Have partnership goals and values been clearly communicated to each task force?
- ❑ Are task forces given a large degree of autonomy? Is bureaucratic control kept to a minimum?
- ❑ Do individual task force participants feel empowered? Are they encouraged to contribute ideas and problem-solving approaches which can then be acted upon?
- ❑ Are task forces encouraged to work collaboratively with each other and with partner institutions?
- ❑ Are task forces and committees reinforced, encouraged and overtly recognized in overall partnership activities, in management meetings, in newsletters and the like?
- ❑ Is individual involvement in task forces recorded and recognized in project reports and in formal and informal acknowledgement processes?
- ❑ Are the task forces and committees open to change and development according to the needs of the constituency(ies) being served?

CHAPTER 6

Developing a Model for Student Support Services

The face of the nation is changing . . . By the year 2020, one-third of the nation will be minority, including Asian Americans. By the last quarter of the 21st century, largely as a result of immigration and differing birth rates, we are projected to be in the majority. It is a change for which the nation is not prepared (Quality Education for Minorities Project Jan., 1990, 11).

- *How can partnerships help with academic advisement?*
- *How can a partnership involve parents?*
- *How can a partnership stimulate the interest of minority students in teaching?*
- *STEP/Outreach Services*

DESPITE their growing numerical status, the thirteen million minority students currently serviced by the U.S. educational system are not faring well. The "Quality Education for Minorities (QEM) Project," funded by the Carnegie Corporation of New York, has recently demonstrated that minority students are half a term behind academically by third grade and a full school year behind by sixth grade, a pattern which has existed for over two decades. The report stresses the need for continuity in educational support services and academic opportunities from pre-school through college and it offers a variety of specific educational initiatives to meet the needs of minority students.

Another current report, funded by the Western Interstate Commission for Higher Education, ***A Crucial Agenda: Making Colleges and Universities Work Better for Minority Students*** (1989), also stresses the need for colleges and universities to play a larger role in supporting the education of minority students through the entire K-12 and higher educational continuum. It cites the difficulties experienced by postsecondary institutions, particularly four year colleges, in attracting and maintaining minority students, especially in such areas as computer science, engineering, business and teacher education. The report specifically recommends the formation of academic and business partnerships and it argues that programs must focus on non-academic as well as on academic influences on minority achievement. In order to encourage minority students to pursue educational opportunities beyond high school, and to become educators themselves, the report argues that educators at both the K-12 and the postsecondary level must address such non-academic factors as unfamiliarity with the world of higher education, fear of failure, cultural background, socialization and parental support. A significant theme of the report is that programs which have successfully assisted underrepresented minority students are consistently multi-dimensional; they employ strategies designed to strengthen students' academic skills, their ability to function in the campus environment, and their self-esteem, sense of purpose, and cultural awareness (*A Crucial Agenda*).

Project STEP is highlighted by this WICHE report as an exemplary model for academic partnerships which specifically address both the academic and non-academic needs of minority students. From the inception of Project STEP, the development of a continuum of support services for students and parents has been considered crucial to the academic advancement of the students.

In the Preface to *A Crucial Agenda,* the authors offer three principal reasons why postsecondary institutions have had relatively little success in attracting and retaining minority students:

1. The underlying problems have not been sufficiently understood;

2. Only small percentages of faculty and staff are expected to give special attention to at-risk minority students;

3. Postsecondary educational institutions and elementary and secondary (K-12) schools have not worked together nearly enough in addressing the underlying problems.

Project STEP provides a model for the type of comprehensive approach recommended by the WICHE report. From the initiation of the partnership, support services for students and parents were considered extremely important. Some of these support services, such as tutoring, were already utilized and institutionalized at the postsecondary level, but only sporadically used by the K-12 schools. Some of the other services, particularly those oriented towards parents, were typically innovative to both secondary and postsecondary institutions and were often of unique importance to the successful integration of minority students into academically oriented programs.

This chapter outlines some of the basic elements which should be considered for inclusion within a multi-dimensional program of support for students and parents. It addresses the following four topics of particular relevance to partnerships serving underrepresented students in depth:

- the nature and components of a comprehensive guidance program;
- how to develop a peer tutoring program;
- methods for encouraging parental interest and support of student academic achievement; and
- approaches for stimulating the interest of underrepresented minorities in teaching.

A model of Project STEP Outreach Services is included at the end of the chapter to illustrate some of the support services currently offered to students and their families through Project STEP.

Students

How can partnerships help with academic advisement?

As one teacher from Santa Ana High School commented in a letter of support for a proposal for external funding associated with the partnership, "My students are very capable, but by and large they have low self-esteem when it comes to envisioning themselves as scholars at major universities." An early goal of Project STEP was to provide a continuum of student support services.

In a presentation made to the Board of Regents of the University of California, Manuel Gomez, Director of Project STEP, illustrated how STEP assists students from the elementary grades through high school by highlighting a few of the programs the partnership offers:

> In elementary school, the child participates, with his or her parents, in a program coordinated by professors from California State University, Fullerton called Family Math/Science, originally developed by the Lawrence Laboratory. The parents are taught games that will increase the child's problem-solving skills and reduce the anxiety often experienced with the learning of mathematics and science. Parents become familiar with the role of technology and good academic preparation for their children's future career options.
>
> In intermediate school, a student joins the Junior High Partnership program with other peers interested in preparing for the university. Parents will join the Parents in Partnership organization and ultimately earn "diplomas" of their own from the UCI "Parent Institute." Programs for peer and parental support continue into each of the high schools in the district, and are reinforced by the Cooperative Learning/ Tutorial Services Program coordinated by Rancho Santiago Community College for all three high schools.

> In their senior year of high school, students receive an analysis of their transcripts by the UCI Admissions Office regarding UC eligibility. Individual follow-up is provided by UCI staff to assist in the University applications procedure.
>
> I believe you now have a better understanding of why we call STEP a "comprehensive" model of intersegmental collaboration, and a "partnership for the advancement of learning" (Manuel Gomez, ***Presentation to the University of California Board of Regents,*** Los Angeles, CA: 1989).

In the early stages of the partnership, during a "brainstorming session" in a Forum entitled *Focus on the Future,* a "wish list" of activities for STEP to sponsor in the next few years was produced. Under the category of student support initiatives, the list included the following:

- teaching students how to set goals which would be translatable into personal academic action plans;

- developing a system for tracking students' academic plans and monitoring their progress according to their plans;

- developing a student handbook for college preparation;

- establishing intermediate and high school academic clubs to enhance educational aspirations and develop a peer support group for these aspirations;

- encouraging minority students, beginning at the intermediate level, to consider teaching as a career through such organizations as "Future Teacher Clubs";

- funding summer program opportunities that encourage leadership and academic achievement;

- developing a "Saturday for Science" series;

- assisting in the development of a district Science Fair;

- developing tutoring programs;

- conducting SAT and ACT preparation and career planning workshops;

- offering cultural awareness events through collaboration with postsecondary Fine Arts Departments;

- providing inservice training for all high school faculty and disseminating information related to college advisement.

Each of these ideas has been developed since the Forum was held, some into full comprehensive programs of their own. For example, the Santa Ana district's Comprehensive Guidance Curriculum, which was initiated under the auspices of STEP support in 1985, is now a fully institutionalized program at each of the secondary schools. It spans grades six through twelve and provides for counselors to teach a set of five guidance lessons in the classroom over the course of each year.

The STEP Task Force on Student Outreach, convened in October 1989, has prepared a matrix descriptive of current student services that includes many of the ideas listed above and more. The matrix (presented at the end of this chapter), demonstrates the coordination necessary in a multi-dimensional program of support for all of the students in the district. The next major activity of this Task Force will be to prepare additional charts that provide a "road map" illustrating the involvement of college and university students and faculty from STEP partner institutions in many of these as well as other activities and programs.

Tutorial Services

> [California Academic Partnership] Projects found involvement of underrepresented students to be most effective when special tutoring efforts were established (Galligani 1987, 31).

Principals at each of the school sites consider the Cooperative Learning Labs (peer tutoring services) to be one of the most important elements of Project STEP. Principals uniformly noted that the Cooperative Learning Labs were valuable both for the students tutored and those involved in providing tutoring services, a finding consistent with over two decades of research on this topic. The goal of this component is to raise the level of achievement of minority students, particularly in the areas of mathematics and science, and to foster minority student interest in teaching.

The establishment of an effective peer-tutoring program such as this requires a partnership to:

- develop a needs assessment instrument to identify student tutoring needs;
- develop a model of tutoring strategies;
- train students to tutor in the designated areas;
- train students to tutor in the range of study skills necessary to achieve success in college;
- coordinate with classroom teachers;
- develop a procedure for referral of students to be tutors
- provide for supervision of tutors by postsecondary faculty and/or students;
- establish mechanisms of student recognition (including salaries, if possible);

- evaluate the effectiveness of the tutorial services and the associated delivery system.

Involvement of Parents/Families

> [California Academic Partnership] Projects indicated that the involvement of parents was extremely critical to enhancing the accomplishments of the underrepresented students involved. If parents were well informed about students' needs as well as sensitive to the project's efforts, they made a positive contribution to the overall success of the project (Galligani 1987, 32).

A central aspect of Project STEP's initiatives has been the focus on parental and family involvement. Two significant activities that have drawn the parents of underrepresented minority students into the academic environment have been the Parents in Partnerships Program and the Family Math Program. Both projects have been extremely successful.

How can a Partnership Involve Parents?

The STEP Project has sponsored a variety of initiatives to engage and empower parents to assist in their children's pursuit of academic goals. Under the Parents in Partnership Program, a component of the UCI EOP/SAA--Outreach Office, activities have included the following:

- PARENT RECEPTIONS--Early evening sessions which have provided specific information on available services provided by the Educational Opportunity and/or Student Affirmative Action programs of the various participating post-secondary institutions;

- WORKSHOPS--Special interest group sessions conducted two to four times during the academic year: topics ranged from "Parenting in the 90's" to

"What's After High School," and "Money for College."

- FAMILY CAREER PLANNING WORKSHOP--Parents and students have learned how to analyze the results of the ACT/CPP (American College Testing/Career Planning Program) career assessment program so they have a clear understanding of the various career possibilities suggested for each student to explore, which are based on each student's indicated experience, abilities, interests, and the level of educational attainment they plan to achieve.

- BILINGUAL NEWSLETTER--With support from the College Board, a newsletter has been published three times a year in Spanish and English. It has provided information about university requirements, useful study and parenting hints, and upcoming activities for parents and students.

- CONFERENCES--These large group sessions, typically sponsored by a countywide regional consortium, have provided information on general topics relevant to the educational development of underrepresented students.

- SOCIAL ACTIVITIES--Including such popular events as the annual Picnic in the Park which features a competition for "Men Who Cook," these activities have been designed to encourage parent/student interaction and to help build stronger relationships and rapport among parents, program staff and students.

- CAMPUS TOURS--Parents and their children have been welcomed by the partner institutions in sponsored trips and campus tours which are designed to excite student interest in attending college, to "demystify" the postsecondary settings and familiarize the parents and students with staff and faculty, and to further encourage involvement of parents in their children's educational activities and progress.

During the past year, a formal Parents in Partnership Foundation was established, which is directed by parents and program coordinators and serves to involve parents in actively raising scholarship funds for students in the school district. This focus on parental involvement has had strikingly positive results. Attendance of high school parents at parent receptions and other activities rose initially from 5% to 25% of the students being represented by a parent and/or family members. With the help of university students who make personal telephone calls to invite parents to upcoming activities, the attendance has now been maintained at the 30% level since 1987, which translates to a group of 400 active "Parents in Partnership" each year.

What is involved in establishing a Family Math Program?

The goal of the Family Math program in Project STEP has been to involve parents of elementary age children in mathematics instruction and to develop a positive school/home relationship that will continue throughout the student's school career. The program was adapted for the partnership from the UC Berkeley Lawrence Hall of Science project of the same name.

The key stages in implementing the program involve the following steps:

- train teachers at the elementary level to lead workshops for parents;

- introduce the program to parents at an Open House or Back-to-School Night at the beginning of the school year;

- conduct weekly sessions for a six-week period, utilizing engaging activities, such as logic games, designed to familiarize parents with the mathematics instruction that their children are receiving in the classroom and to assist them in developing mathematics and problem-solving skills at home.

The concept of family-based instruction has been so successful that individual teachers at the elementary schools involved subsequently developed "Family Computer" programs, and plan to develop and incorporate within the program a "Family Science" component. Moreover, the Family Math program has been recommended for institutionalization by the school-district LEP (Limited-English Proficient) Student Task Force. In recommending the program for institutionalization, the LEP report noted that "the Family Math Program offered opportunities to parents and teachers to learn collaborative methods for helping LEP students."

How can a partnership stimulate the interest of minority students in teaching?

The need for bilingual teachers and teachers sensitive to multicultural and multilingual classrooms is a pressing one for Project STEP's partner school district. It is also increasingly a problem of both the present and the future for many school districts. Project STEP has targeted the following groups from which to attract for future bilingual and minority teachers:

- the students in the school district;
- the teacher aides in the school district;
- the undergraduate students and the teacher credential candidates involved in teacher training programs in partnership institutions; and
- also the undergraduates in general, for recruitment of students to orientation sessions by the offices of teacher education.

STEP has used the following approaches to stimulate interest in teaching in K-12 students:

- "Future Teacher Clubs";
- peer tutoring opportunities;
- exposure to role-models through presentations by post-secondary faculty who are themselves underrepresented minorities.

Among teachers and the Project has stimulated interest and provided opportunities in pursuing the teaching profession through the following approaches:

- providing workshops for bilingual aides to share with them information regarding college and university admissions requirements and procedures, financial aid resources and programs, and the content and requirements of programs leading to a teaching credential.
- developing follow-up campus visits and providing release time, thereby enabling bilingual aides to become familiar with postsecondary institutions and programs of interest to them;
- creating a "Teachers of Tomorrow" club involving bilingual aides;
- inviting aides who are interested in pursuing teaching careers to attend STEP workshops for district teachers focused on a range of instructional topics.

STEP has stimulated interest among teacher education candidates in teaching within minority school districts through such approaches as the following:

- inviting outstanding district bilingual teachers to give demonstration lessons for undergraduate teacher education students and creating videotapes of those lessons for subsequent use; and

- creating a "fast-track" whereby outstanding teacher education students can be hired into the district partner school.

A major contribution of Project STEP to furthering minority student interest in teaching, beyond offering the experience of working with students in the Cooperative Learning Laboratory components, has been its focus on providing teachers with opportunities for personal academic enrichment and professional growth. As K-12 teachers have revitalized their own interest in and enthusiasm for teaching, so a career in teaching becomes a more attractive possibility for students.

STEP/OUTREACH SERVICES ELEMENTARY GRADES

Program/Activity	Description	Contact(s)/Institution(s)
College Tours 5th Grade	Fifth grade students from all elementary schools in Santa Ana are taken on tours of Rancho Santiago College.	- Rancho Santiago College
La Escuelita	A community service project from UCI for tutoring in school. This project also can include community awareness field trips for students.	- UC Irvine
Saturdays for Science Grades 4 - 6	Series of 4 one-hour introductory science programs.	- UC Irvine
4-H Club Youth Program (University of California Cooperative Extension)	Develop leadership skills in students through projects and activities.	- UC Irvine
Career Day	Professionals from various occupations speak to students and visit classrooms.	- Rancho Santiago College - Cal State, Fullerton - UC Irvine
4-H Parent Training	Six-week leadership training program.	- UC Irvine
Parent Institute	Symposium held at CSUF to educate parents on the various service programs available throughout the state (Note: Available to all grades and levels).	- Cal State, Fullerton
Parent Education	Classes for parents in *Beginning ESL, Positive Parenting*, etc.	- Rancho Santiago College

STEP/OUTREACH SERVICES INTERMEDIATE GRADES

Program/Activity	Description	Contact(s)/Institution(s)
8th Grade Presentation	A college motivational presentation given to all eighth graders at a school site to inform them of their post-secondary educational options.	- UC Irvine
Parent Conference (District-wide Activity) 8th Grade	A one-day conference designed to provide parents with information on various topics not addressed at the parent workshops.	- UC Irvine
Leadership Conference (District-wide Activity) 8th Grade	A one-day Saturday leadership development conference designed to assist EAO participants to develop leadership skills.	- UC Irvine
ACT Career Assessment 8th Grade	A three-hour Career Assessment test for EAO participants. This activity includes a parent night to follow-up with results of the test.	- UC Irvine
UC eligibility Plan Assistance (New Program 1989-90) Grade 8	Meet with EAO eighth graders to develop a one-year high school enrollment plan.	- UC Irvine
Junior High Partnership Program	Academic club for students interested in preparing for postsecondary education.	- UC Irvine
Future Teachers Club	Club for students interested in becoming teachers.	- Santa Ana Unified School District
Peer Tutoring Program	High school and intermediate students are trained to tutor their peers.	- Rancho Santiago College
Parents in Partnership	Continued workshops and informational meetings. Parent newsletter.	- UC Irvine/Educational Opportunity Program

STEP/OUTREACH SERVICES GRADES 9 - 12

Program/Activity	Description	Contact(s)/Institution(s)
UC Partners Program (Early Outreach)	A variety of activities are done, primarily with underclassmen. Group presentations and field trips enhance college awareness.	- UC Irvine
STEP Club (Community Service)	Extra-curricular program which strengthens critical thinking skills through the exploration of current social issues. Meetings are conducted seminar-style and utilize the media (*i.e.* newspaper/magazine articles, films, etc.) as its primary resource.	- UC Irvine
Artist in Training	Music, dance, and drama presentations delivered by Fine Arts UCI students.	- UC Irvine
Visiting Professors Program	Lectures given by professors. Students are given related reading assignments prior to the lecture.	- UC Irvine - Cal State, Fullerton - Rancho Santiago College
Credit by Exam	High school students are given competency exams in designated subjects with the possibility of earning course credit.	- Rancho Santiago College
Vocational Tours	Tours of vocational subject classrooms are given to high school Regional Occupational Program students.	- Rancho Santiago College
Scholarship Foundation (New Program 1989-90) Grades 8 - 12	A parental effort to solicit community monies to enable the SAUSD to provide college scholarships to its students.	- UC Irvine
MESA (Mathematics, Engineering, Science Achievement)	School clubs to bring together students and encourage interest in science/math careers, especially minority students.	- Cal State, Fullerton - UC Irvine
MESA Field Trips	Students tour local industries to stimulate interest in science or mathematics-related careers.	- Cal State, Fullerton

STEP/OUTREACH SERVICES
GRADE 10

Program/Activity	Description	Contact(s)/Institution(s)
College Walkabout	Students visit a college campus, but instead of doing the typical tour we pair our students up with college students. They spend the day with their college hosts, attending classes, having lunch, going to the bookstore, and so forth. There may be some group activities as well, but the real emphasis is on sampling college life with a "real-life" college student. (NOTE: This activity could include 11th and 12th grade students.)	- Cal State, Long Beach - UC Irvine - UC Riverside
Early Outreach Counseling	Ninth and tenth grade students are given group presentations to increase their awareness of the various options open to them. This is frequently done in *High School Planning* classes.	- Cal State, Fullerton - UC Irvine - Rancho Santiago College
College Majors Faire Grades 10-11	A one-day Majors and Career Awareness forum involving teachers, counselors, and university students designed to awaken students' knowledge of a particular major or career choice.	- UC Irvine

STEP/OUTREACH SERVICES GRADE 11

Program/Activity	Description	Contact(s)/Institution(s)
College Planning Week	Classes come to the Career Center for one week during the spring in order to prepare juniors for the college application. The schedule and topics are modified each year to meet the needs of the students and to take advantage of college presentations. The last day is a College Options Showcase.	- UC Irvine - Cal State, Fullerton - Rancho Santiago College - Chapman College
SAT Workshop	A Saturday SAT Prep Workshop, as well as summer workshops.	- UC Irvine
Transcript Review	A systematic review of the transcripts of freshmen, sophomores, and juniors to assist them to achieve UC or Cal-State eligibility.	- UC Irvine - Cal State Fullerton
KSR Summer Program (Knowledge and Social Responsibility)	A ten-day honors summer residential program designed to academically, socially, and intellectually challenge high school juniors.	- UC Irvine
PCATS (Peer Counseling & Academic Training Symposium)	One-week residential program designed to train high school students to assist other students with the college and financial aid application process.	- UC Irvine
College Day	Junior students are invited to RSC for an orientation to the campus. Food, tours, and advisement are provided. Junior students spend a day at UCI and are oriented to classes and campus life.	- Rancho Santiago College - UC Irvine
UCI EAO Stay Over Program	A week-end program for top juniors designed to give them a realistic view of college life through direct interaction with university students.	- UC Irvine

STEP/OUTREACH SERVICES
GRADE 12

Program/Activity	Description	Contact(s)/Institution(s)
On-site College Representative	A paid student or adult representative from the college maintains regular hours on the high school campus for the purpose of assisting with college applications or financial aid, doing class presentations to disseminate general information, or acting as a tutor.	- Rancho Santiago College - Cal State, Fullerton - UC Irvine - CAL-SOAP (California Student Opportunity & Access Program)
College Application Workshops	Group workshops held at individual school sites to assist large groups of students complete their college applications.	- UC Irvine - Cal State, Fullerton - Rancho Santiago College - Chapman College - CAL-SOAP - UC Riverside
Field Evaluation Program	Representatives from all UC undergraduate campuses meet with students individually.	- UC Irvine
Placement Testing and Applications	All seniors who had indicated an interest in the community college are given the required placement test.	- Rancho Santiago College
Financial Aid Workshops/ Students	Students are brought together for a two-day session on financial aid applications. Representatives from the community college, Cal State, UC, and private schools assist the seniors.	- UC Irvine - Cal State, Fullerton - Rancho Santiago College - Chapman College - CAL-SOAP
Financial Aid Workshop/ Parents	Evening workshops are designed to provide parents and students with assistance in completing the SAAC forms.	- UC Irvine
Career Beginnings	Mentors from the business community meet regularly with students to develop and motivate career interests and college entrance. Summer employment results for the students as well as possible college scholarships.	- Rancho Santiago College

STEP/OUTREACH SERVICES POSTSECONDARY

Program/Activity	Description	Contact(s)/Institution(s)
Articulation Conference in K-12 Language Arts Framework	Community college instructors attended inservice workshops by K-12 language arts instructors.	- Rancho Santiago College
Bilingual Teaching Presentations for Teacher Education Faculty and Students	Bilingual teachers taught methodologies for the bilingual and multicultural classroom. Videotapes were made for teacher education faculty at other institutions.	- UC Irvine
Visiting Scholar Program	An extramurally funded project jointly developed by UC Irvine, OCC and SAUSD to facilitate the formation of discipline-based academic alliances. A course for interinstitutional collaboration developed for national dissemination.	- UC Irvine - Orange Coast College - Santa Ana Unified School District
Teacher Aide Conferences	Annual conferences for district instructional aides to help prepare them for teaching careers.	- UC Irvine - CSU Fullerton - Rancho Santiago College
Teacher Aide Campus Visits and Counseling	Visits to individual campuses to meet with faculty, academic counselors, financial aid staff and administrators and plan individual courses of study.	- UC Irvine - CSU Fullerton - Rancho Santiago College
Linguistic Minority Bilingual Laserdisc Research Project	A collaborative research and demonstration project testing bilingual videodiscs for teaching advanced science to limited English proficient students.	- UC Irvine - Santa Ana Unified School District
Kids Network (Global Common Classroom Project)	Several college faculty, student teachers, secondary principals and 4th-6th grade teachers implemented a collaborative research and demonstration project establishing telecommunications between classrooms in Santa Ana and the Soviet Union.	- UC Irvine - Santa Ana Unified School District

CHAPTER 7

Evaluating Partnerships

Inquiry is the . . . directed transformation of an indeterminate situation into one that is so determinate in its constitutent distinctions and relations as to convert the elements of the original situation into a unified whole (John Dewey 1938).

- *Key points in designing partnership evaluation*
- *Using a range of approaches for evaluating partnerships*
- *Evaluation as a process: the example of participation rates*
- *Taking advantage of routine institutional evaluation and data collection activities*
- *The scope of partnership evaluations*
- *Evaluating organizational change*
- *Assessing changes in "climates of belief" and in expectations and attitudes*
- *Making evaluation results useful to partnership members*
- *Evaluation Checklist*

THIS CHAPTER is intended to serve as a tool for individuals involved in evaluating intersegmental partnerships in education. It is designed to provide general guidance concerning the variety of methods for evaluating partnerships and suggestions for evaluating both the progress and impact of partnerships. Its focus is on the unique attributes of part-nership evaluations. Much additional information relevant to evaluation of partnerships is found within the general field of educational program evaluation.

Key Points in Designing Partnership Evaluation

In designing the evaluation of intersegmental partnerships, several key points need to be emphasized. They are as follow:

1. There is *no single best approach* to partnership evaluation. What is important is that a variety of evaluation methods be used which are responsive to the partnership goals, typically some internal and some involving external, objective third-party assessment.

2. Evaluation is a *process* which should be part of the ongoing management of a partnership and its activities, not an independent activity separated from other components of the partnership.

3. The *routine evaluation and data collection activities* conducted by participating school districts and institutions of higher education provide valuable information for partnership evaluation.

4. Evaluations should include *qualitative as well as quantitative* data. They should document *implementation and process effects as well as outcomes*. They should examine *intended as well as unanticipated* outcomes.

5. Many of the effects of partnerships are subtle and relate to *organizational behavior*. A variety of *unobtrusive indicators* reflecting ways in which school and university activities are being conducted and have been changed are of particular value in measuring organizational outcomes.

6. Changes in *"climates of belief"* and in *expectations and attitudes* of partnership members regarding what is possible in K-12 schools and in postsecondary education may be among the most lasting effects and should not be overlooked.

7. Evaluations of partnerships must address *long-term and sustained impacts* as well as immediately measurable effects.

8. Evaluation results should be *made available on a timely and continuous basis* for use by partnership members in decision-making and in planning strategies for addressing student, parent, teachers and other school personnel needs in relation to enhancing educational success.

Using a Range of Approaches For Evaluating Partnerships

Internal Evaluation

The STEP Partnership has from its inception considered the ongoing collection of evaluation information to be extremely important. By way of example, STEP has each year compiled information concerning participation rates in project activities, teachers' and parents' opinions about these activities, student application and enrollment data in institutions of higher education, and costs of project components. These data have been collected as part of the project's internal evaluation. They have been extremely valuable in identifying project successes and in determining what additional steps are needed to accomplish project goals.

Examples from the data collected by Project STEP about Component #3: *Family Mathematics for Kindergarten through Sixth Grade,* are illustrative of the variety of indicators used for monitoring project implementation and effects. Information concerning K-6 teachers and administrators involved in Family Math Training Workshops as well as about the Santa Ana schools which they represented was collected. The involvement of intermediate school staff was considered essential to success of the component, and their participation (including teachers, guidance staff and administrators) was documented as a distinct part of the evaluation. Further, the number of students and parents who participated in the Family Math sessions and their distinct part of the evaluation. Further, the number of students and parents who participated in the Family Math sessions and their distribution by ethnicity was documented. The pooling of resources involved in the conduct of the Family Math sessions and the costs of this project component were also documented. Comments of parents were recorded and used to provide feedback to project staff and included such statements as the following:

> *The best part of the class is making math fun like a game and having us as parents visualize math and see it drawn on the screen. It helped a lot rather than just reading it on paper.*
>
> *You could make the class longer.*
>
> *Continue having these classes--children need to learn math.*

Consistent with the emphasis on comprehensive evaluation, an array of information has been collected for each Project STEP component. In most instances, while the collection of a breadth of information has been planned in advance, additional indicators have also been identified during project implementation. For each project component, sample activities, participation rates, student learning and other outcome measures, and potential measurement strategies were identified both during the planning of STEP operations and on an ongoing basis. This was extremely helpful both in terms of identifying valid measures for assessing project success and for involving and communicating to teachers and other participants evaluation strategies and results.

A clear lesson from Project STEP is that the internal evaluation procedures a partnership will use must be planned in advance but also be responsive to suggestions of participants in order to be effective. While this may often be the case with any educational program, it is particularly important in a partnership. First, partnership activities by their very nature are complex. It is quite possible to document them and their effects thoroughly while they are in progress, but it is extremely difficult either to do so without the involvement of participants or to reconstruct such events accurately after they have been concluded. Further, the choice and administration of data collection procedures can either enhance or harm the partnership. *If each of the parties has not had the opportunity to contribute to decisions about evaluation measures or has not been consulted concerning procedures for collecting data, misunderstandings and intrusions can result which may adversely affect the entire partnership and its functioning.*

External Evaluation

External evaluation has also been an integral component of Project STEP. Through it, the Administrative Council has received objective feedback about the features of the partnership which have contributed to its effectiveness, the features which make it unique, and activities which it might consider doing differently. The third-party evaluators have been thoroughly impartial, providing an independent view of Project STEP which participants themselves or an internal evaluator would be unlikely to be able to provide.

The comments by one group of external evaluators, in a report prepared for the College Board, are an example of ways in which objective, third-party evaluation has contributed to an understanding of Project STEP in ways which add significantly to the perceptions of those directly involved in the project. The report of the external evaluators identified a number of the factors explaining the success of Project STEP. By way of example, the report indicated the following:

> . . . The most critical factor [in the success of Project STEP] . . . is the almost universal commitment to action which was revealed in the site visit. Participants know the literature, they know the local conditions, they see the future and they agree that they want to do something. This pervasive attitude on the part of a small core group of leaders seems to be rippling out to include an ever increasing circle of teachers, parents, and administrators within the school district and professors and administrators at the four colleges and universities in the area.

> The second most striking feature is the extensive local, state, and national connections project leaders tap to support STEP activities . . . . each participant was extensively involved in other pursuits that brought them into contact with a wide range of people who might also be important to STEP success. They shared this information easily, almost casually, yet it was the kind of information that would open doors to needed expertise and fiscal resources (Van de Water 1989, 19-20).

Third party, objective evaluations do not, of course, serve primarily to communicate project successes. They also identify areas that warrant more attention. In the case of Project STEP, it was of particular value to have an independent evaluation which addressed goals not yet fully accomplished. The comments of evaluators who assessed each of the projects within the California Academic Partnership Program (CAPP) underscored for the STEP Administrative Council and various staff the importance of focusing additional attention and resources on *institutionalization and dissemination*--two critical ingredients if partnerships are to have *lasting and broadly-based impacts*.

In summary, while there is no one best strategy for evaluating a partnership, some points should be kept in mind. It is necessary to use a variety of data collection techniques in order to assess the array of process and outcome effects which relate to the project's goals. In addition, much value comes from conducting both ongoing internal evaluation and periodic external evaluation.

Evaluation as a Process: The Example of Participation Rates

In understanding evaluation as a process, it is useful to recognize that evaluation activities should typically be helpful to the various participants involved in a partnership. Evaluations of intersegmental partnership activities should serve not only K-12 and postsecondary administrative staff but also teachers, aides, school principals, curriculum developers, parents and college and university faculty if they are to be supportive of significant goals. By incorporating the informational needs of various participants into the design and conduct of evaluations, one can increase the likelihood that ongoing assessments will address the questions these groups need and want answered in order to enhance their effectiveness within the partnership.

Project STEP has consistently used a number of forms of evaluation to provide feedback to participants, making evaluation an integral part of the project. As noted above, readily available indicators have been used to track the number and percent of teachers, guidance counselors, administrators, students and parents who participate in each project component, often providing data by grade level, ethnicity and/or gender. This enables school district and college and university representatives to determine whether all or only some groups of staff, students and parents are being selected for or choosing to take part in project opportunities. By way of illustration, STEP annual reports indicate how many students from which schools and at which grade levels have participated in Tutoring, in the Junior High Partnership, and in the various High School Programs. Because the data are reported each year, they provide continuous feedback which can be used by the Administrative Council for management purposes.

In order to make such evaluation activities as documentation of participation in project activities an integral project management tool, assessment must be carried out *consistently* and *from the beginning* of project activities. Much data can be collected relatively inexpensively if this information collection is built into project activities. It is a straightforward matter to describe project activities, but it does require advanced planning and organization. In order for the collection of project data to assist and not interfere with partnership activities, this information should be collected in as simple and efficient a way as possible (e.g., sign-in sheets, analyses of agendas and minutes, videotaping of events, etc.) and reported to managers on a designated schedule in a manner which is readily interpretable and easy to use.

In summary, evaluation can and should be made an element of partnership activities and management. Intersegmental partnerships are intrinsically multifaceted phenomena. It is of great value to have multiple sources of feedback about them for administrators and participants to be able to use in decision-making and program implementation. Participation and cost data are examples of valuable sources of information which can be obtained readily and which can increase the likelihood that evaluation will become a component of ongoing partnership management--informing decisions on a continuing basis--but which are often overlooked.

Taking Advantage of Routine Institutional Evaluation and Data Collection Activities

Making use of the wide array of measures collected by the participating entities within intersegmental partnerships helps to avoid one of the potential pitfalls of evaluation--data collection activities and costs which cannot be sustained. This point is particularly true for partnerships between K-12 and postsecondary educational institutions. As a result of the variety of accountability requirements which most school districts must address, a considerable amount of information is typically collected each year. Similarly, colleges and universities collect and report a wide range of application, enrollment and performance information each year. For intersegmental partnerships, the combination of these different sources of information provides a series of distinct and complementary views of the functioning and impacts of partnership activities.

Many examples of the richness of routinely collected school district data can be seen within STEP evaluation activities. Student achievement results on commercial tests administered by the District each year, student performance on annual statewide tests, attendance and truancy data, students' scores on college entrance tests, the number of students taking such tests, the numbers applying to each of the segments of higher education, and the performance of project students within postsecondary institutions--these are all examples of the types of data which are useful for evaluating project effects. By examining the relationship between individual student and school site participation in STEP activities and these outcome indicators, project managers can determine the relative effectiveness of a variety of program components in relation to various outcomes.

Similarly, *information routinely collected and reported by colleges and universities has great potential for providing useful feedback to project managers.* Data from application and admission files, student undergraduate course enrollments, students' grades and persistence in postsecondary education, their participation in academic support activities (e.g., tutoring, study skills assistance, etc.) as part of their postsecondary education--indicators such as these can help to identify lasting impacts and areas needing additional attention at the elementary and secondary school levels.

In summary, there are many sources of already collected and readily available information which can assist in evaluating partnerships. Constructing a "collage" of such data sources enables managers and project participants to receive rich feedback concerning partnership activities without requiring significant and unsustainable evaluation costs.

The Scope of Partnership Evaluations

There are three key issues which managers should keep in mind in order to make partnership evaluations maximally useful. The first concerns the nature of evaluation measures for assessing partnerships: indicators must include qualitative as well as quantitative measures. On the one hand, it is essential that specific objectives be stated in relation to measurable outcomes. This means that quantitative indicators are generally necessary for assessing progress. At the same time, many of the fundamental institutional changes which must occur for partnerships to have significant and sustained impacts require qualitative measures. These may take the form of interviews, of systematic observations of partnership meetings and activities, of logs prepared by participants, or of reports by external individuals. The procedures for collecting qualitative data likely will vary in relation to available resources and opportunities; what project managers must recognize is the importance of qualitative information and of assuring that it is collected.

Related to this issue is the importance of collecting implementation and process data as well as outcome data. The implementation of activities will be the foundation for their success or failure. Because implementation is not readily observable to all partnership members, it needs to be documented as a basis for shared reflection on project progress. Further, the measure of a partnership's benefits is often found as much in process changes as in outcomes. If, for example, faculty from a college or university are spending time at school sites, are participating in workshops for K-12 teachers, students or parents, and are meeting with K-12 representatives to discuss preparation for postsecondary education, their participation is real. If this is not occurring, it may be a stated goal experiencing little realization. Documenting what is actually occurring as part of the partnership is critical for identifying and understanding goal attainment and areas needing further effort.

Finally, it is essential to examine unanticipated as well as intended outcomes. Examples of unanticipated outcomes in Project STEP have included the following:

- Project STEP's rosters of student participants have been used to invite pupils to participate in Summer Pre-Algebra Institutes conducted by institutions of higher education;

- Graduates of Santa Ana's high schools have been systematically contacted, enabling the District to demonstrate its interest in these young peoples' future progress and to provide information about postsecondary opportunities to them;

- Principals at STEP schools have been invited to participate in regional Principal-to-Principal professional development institutes;

- New collaborative relationships have been established between Santa Ana, business and industry representatives, and individuals in leadership positions within the fields of science education, school-based applications of educational technologies and addressing the needs of high-risk youth (e.g., through gang suppression, drug abuse prevention, etc.);

- New relationships have been established between Santa Ana and postsecondary institutions in the region. These have resulted in added career advancement opportunities in education for bilingual aides within the District and strengthening of the preparation of teacher candidates in nearby colleges and universities for working within multilingual and multicultural classrooms.

While numerous unanticipated outcomes associated with Project STEP have been positive, it is also possible that unfortunate unanticipated outcomes will be detected in partnerships. It could be, for example, that a result of one partnership is to weaken rather than to strengthen the sense of efficacy and ownership in internal institutional decisions experienced by participants. Or, it could be that a partnership's successes are associated with a weakening of the necessary authority of certain administrators within one or more institution. There are generally ways of dealing with unanticipated outcomes rapidly with the result that problems can be corrected--but it is necessary to identify negative as well as positive unanticipated effects in order to be able to address potential problems as soon as possible.

Evaluating Organizational Change

The most profound impacts of intersegmental partnerships are on organizational behavior. If effective, partnerships between K-12 and postsecondary education will change organizational norms, cultures, and "rituals." They will lead to new informal as well as formal organizational dynamics. They will change the ways in which individuals assess themselves and their roles in relation to the institutions of which they are members. These are subtle and not easily measured influences. How does one measure these organizational changes? The experience of Project STEP has been that this is often best done through both unobtrusive indicators and qualitative components of independent evaluation.

As an example of organizational change associated with Project STEP, one can look at the increased collaboration among various units within the participating entities. At UC Irvine, for example, a substantial amount of cooperation between the Educational Opportunity Program/Student Affirmative Action Office and a variety of departments and schools and among these departments and schools has occurred in conjunction with Project STEP. The Office of Teacher Education, the Department of Mathematics, the Department of Chemistry, and the School of Biological Sciences have all begun working together in the pursuit of STEP goals. Numerous activities--from the joint preparation of proposals for external funding aimed at enhancing preparation of underrepresented students in science and mathematics--to collaboration in community service activities serving significant concentrations of language minority and economically disadvantaged students--reflect this pattern.

Independent evaluations are often useful in assessing changes in organizational behavior. Passages from an evaluation conducted by the College Board are a good illustration of the ways in which a *third-party objective assessment can assist in identifying and describing organizational behavior and change.*

> The formal structure [of Project STEP] is considered necessary because of the multifaceted nature of the project. It provides an avenue for setting priorities and resolving issues. In day-to-day operations, however, little reference is needed to the formal structure because Project STEP has successfully developed a collegial environment in which problems and issues are typically resolved through informal discussion and consensus.
>
> The STEP components provide an opportunity to collaborate within the school district and across educational levels. School district leaders welcome collaboration as a two-way learning vehicle which makes additional resources, both people and money,

> available to the district. Postsecondary participants are excited about the opportunity to learn about the issues facing secondary schools and work with their secondary colleagues to better prepare students for college entrance and success.
>
> seek out and respond to school site initiatives. The newly formed teacher advisory committee, as one example, provides an avenue for teachers to recommend new ideas and directions to the administrative council (Van de Water 1989, 20-22).

The collection of qualitative data addressing organizational behavior and changes within independent evaluations does not need to be costly. What needs to occur is that independent evaluators are alerted to the importance of this dimension to project administrators as they design, plan for and conduct their work.

Assessing Changes in "Climates of Belief" and in Expectations and Attitudes

Successful partnerships generally have an institutional "Pygmalion" effect. Such partnerships typically alter individuals' perceptions about what is possible--both what is possible within their own institutions and in intersegmental collaboration. The "climate of belief" changes from one of skepticism and limited expectations to a broader vision seeing significant opportunities as being both possible and valuable.

These changes must not be overlooked, especially because they may be the most important and the most lasting effects of effective partnerships. In order for these changes in "climates of belief" to be measured, baseline indicators must be collected. *Thus, it is important to have interview or questionnaire data collected at some early points in the development of a partnership which capture the feelings of key individuals regarding the possibilities for and benefits of intersegmental collaboration. In addition, it is extremely valuable to have routine minutes prepared of intersegmental partnership meetings in order to assess changes over time.* It is not necessary that extensive information be collected to address this area. Rather, what is important is that (a) minutes and documentation of partnership meetings and activities be recorded on a consistent basis and (b) a select number of carefully designed questions be asked of a range of individuals as a way of capturing initial and subsequent perceptions regarding the potential of partnerships and of the institutions themselves to initiate, effect, and maintain change.

Evaluating Long-Term and Sustained Impacts

If a partnership is successful, it will not be the case that effects are experienced and then begin to diminish within a few months or years. Rather, intersegmental arrangements established and their benefits will grow, change over time, and be sustained. *It is important that the lasting effects of partnerships be examined, both as critical information for participating institutions and as a contribution of the increasing understanding of the dynamics and evolution of intersegmental partnerships in education.*

Measuring sustained and long-term impacts requires a commitment to longitudinal evaluation. When evaluations are designed, they should be viewed not as one or two year ventures, but as efforts which will continue over three, four or five years. If measures have been carefully selected to draw upon readily available indicators, the long-term nature of the evaluation need not make it prohibitively expensive.

Making Evaluation Results Functionally Useful to Partnership Members

It should be understood that the primary users of partnership evaluations are the participants themselves. Institutions enter into intersegmental partnerships because they wish to accomplish goals which they recognize would be difficult if not impossible to achieve alone. The types of institutions and individuals who make the commitments and take the inherent risks associated with partnerships are motivated to make positive changes. Thus, they should be seen as key audiences who will be interested in knowing and using evaluation results. While there will be many other users (including funding agencies, K-12 and postsecondary representatives elsewhere, scholars, etc.), their needs likely can be addressed without compromising the utility of evaluations to partnership numbers themselves.

What is the key to enabling participants to use evaluations both for informing themselves and for improving partnership activities and efforts? A primary ingredient is the following: *making evaluation results available on a timely and continuous basis and in readily interpretable language.* Through this process, feedback can be provided to the many individuals within the various segments of K-12 and postsecondary education who make an investment in collaboration. They need the guidance which only honest "intelligence" can provide in order for them to realize the significant successes which they seek for the youth within their schools.

The following checklist has been developed to assist intersegmental partnerships in designing and conducting evaluations which will be valuable tools in project management and for assessing partnership progress. The checklist is meant to be a convenient method of assuring that critical steps are undertaken in the evaluation-related activities of any partnership between K-12 and postsecondary education.

Evaluation Checklist

- ❑ Evaluation strategies and methods have been selected which are directly responsive to the partnership goals.

- ❑ The evaluation has been designed with the specific intent of assuring that it will be useful to the ongoing management of the partnership and its activities.

- ❑ The evaluation will make use of routine data collection activities conducted by participating school districts and institutions of higher education.

- ❑ The evaluation will include:
  - ❑ Qualitative as well as quantitative data;
  - ❑ Assessment of implementation and process;
  - ❑ Measurement of the range of relevant outcomes;
  - ❑ Attention to unanticipated as well as intended effects.

- ❑ The evaluation will address changes in organizational behaviors.

- ❑ The evaluation will assess changes in "climates of belief" and in expectations and attitudes of partnership members.

- ❑ The evaluation will deal with long-term and sustained impacts as well as immediately measurable effects.

- ❑ Procedures have been developed to assure that evaluation results are made available both (a) on a timely and continuous basis for use by partnership members and (b) to inform external audiences.

CHAPTER 8

Communicating for Partnership Cohesion and Dissemination

A successful partnership becomes a "community of believers" that has a high level of administrative support, realistic goals, and an effective communications system to reach all participants (DeBevoise 1986).

- *What staff communication skills are necessary within partnerships?*
- *What information needs to be communicated?*
- *How can information be communicated internally to teachers, administrators, parents?*
- *How can this information be communicated externally to other partnerships, to the community?*

COMMUNICATION lies at the heart of Project STEP's success and at the heart of most partnership goals. To a larger extent, the initial reason for designing academic partnerships is to overcome a previous lack of effective communication between different sectors of the academic community. Subsequent to a conference of Southern California university and school district representatives, the Assistant to the Superintendent of the Santa Ana Unified School District, Ramon Reza, commented to a local newspaper on the unique level of collaboration within STEP:

> None [of the other partnerships] had as close a communication between a university, a college and a school district as we enjoy (*The Orange County Register,* March 2, 1989).

Robin Casselman, Associate Director of Project STEP, echoed the importance of communication in the same news article:

> There's still the need for more communication. . . . communication keeps teachers and counselors aware of what their colleagues are doing [in each of the STEP partner institutions] (*The Orange County Register,* March 2, 1989).

How, then, can a partnership maintain a high level of communication--critical to commitment--within a partnership?

What Staff Communication Skills are Necessary Within Partnerships?

Communication primarily depends on people. Key staff people must have good communication skills: good interpersonal skills, good verbal communications skills and good writing skills--and must practice these skills consistently with both groups and individuals (Ottenbourg 1986, 177).

Project STEP has been fortunate to retain the same project director and associate director for the first seven years of its existence. Despite some turnover at the school district level, key participants in the project know each other well and have developed a level of informal communication and support that underpins many partnership initiatives. During a California Academic Partnership Program (CAPP) site visit by members of the CAPP Advisory Board to the Santa Ana Unified School District in November 1989, teachers and administrators talked about the sense of "family" within the partnership, the "collegiality between postsecondary and K-12 participants," and the "open lines of communication." One school principal commented on the consistently positive interactions that he had with the project staff, in particular the university project director and associate director. Another principal described how much he valued his feeling of "connection" with the postsecondary sector and the project staff, and indicated that he could "pick up the phone" and discuss problems, ideas and strategies.

This is not to convey the thought that we have not had our conflicts and problems, but we have managed to handle these differences in a positive way. Clearly, a partnership cannot undervalue the importance of interpersonal relationships and communication skills. Otterbourg recommends ongoing staff development for the partnership as a team--with training related to oral and written communication--to improve and solidify both communications skills and positive public perceptions of the partnership as a coordinated and effective program (Otterbourg 1986, 177). Project STEP has not undertaken such training, but rather relied on the tone and expectations established and maintained by project leaders in the conduct of STEP activities.

What Information Needs to Be Communicated?

A partnership must decide what information needs to be communicated and how it should be communicated. Project STEP, like most other partnerships, has five general areas about which communication is often found within partnerships:

1. program administration and management;

2. program planning, development and implementation for activities involving students, staff, and partners;

3. program monitoring and evaluation;

4. recognition of students, staff, and partners for their achievements and contributions (human, material and financial);

5. community awareness and public relations.

An examination of the communication vehicles used for each of these areas reveals significant attention to record keeping and transmission of information within and beyond the partnership.

How Can Information Be Communicated Within the Partnership?

The importance of formal and informal communication to a partnership cannot be overstated. The following section describes a number of successful methods for facilitating and strengthening such communication.

Administrative Council Minutes

Minutes of the Administrative Council meetings of Project STEP have been highly informative and have been disseminated throughout the partnership, particularly to C.E.O.'s, but also to all other partnership leaders. In this way, partner institutions and members are kept informed of the progress of program initiatives, the development of new directions within the partnership, and major opportunities and achievements that contribute to the partnership.

Faculty Forums

One of Project STEP's most innovative communication strategies is the use of Faculty Forums. These are essentially staff development activities, presented in the form of seminars involving considerable dialogue. Outside faculty may share successful ideas and projects related to partnership goals, such as Jaime Escalante talking about motivating minority students in mathematics. Participants may share teaching and guidance strategies used in partnership components, such as interdisciplinary teaching in Mathematics and Science or Critical Thinking Skills and Writing. The tone of these forums is of colleagues sharing ideas, as well as dialoguing with "experts."

Resource Guides

As one of its communication strategies, Project STEP has assisted in the development of school district resource guides--to-date, in the areas of guidance, mathematics, science and language arts. These guides are invaluable tools for faculty and counselors to adapt curricular revisions and new teaching practices designed for practical implementation of the spirit of the California ***Model Curriculum Standards.*** They also serve to enhance institutionalization and themselves illustrate the extent to which the partnership has become institutionalized with the school district.

Newsletters

Through the UCI Educational Opportunity Program, Project STEP disseminates a quarterly newsletter in Spanish and English to parents. This newsletter informs parents about upcoming activities designed particularly for their participation, such as workshops and conferences. It also tells parents about other partnership programs and achievements and generally helps to keep them involved in their children's education. Project STEP is currently devising a routine newsletter for teachers and administrators within the partnership. The fact that the first newsletter was prepared for communication with parents is indicative of the value which has been placed on encouraging their meaningful involvement with the project and with school activities.

Recognition Materials and Events

Recognition of partnership achievements in Project STEP has included publicity concerning student and staff activities, the donation of materials to the project by groups and individuals, the sponsoring of project events, volunteer services, and so forth. Dissemination of information concerning program accomplishments to the larger community serves to express public appreciation for partnership efforts and contributions and to increase knowledge, understanding and support for the partnership within the community.

How Can Information Be Disseminated Beyond the Partnership?

In order to contribute to the increasing body of knowledge about partnerships, each such collaborative needs one or more dissemination strategies. As described below, the strategies can be integrally tied to ongoing partnerships functions and activities.

Annual/Periodic Reports

Since partnerships are usually linked to major funding sources, annual reports become valuable tools for evaluation, as well as serving to inform funding agencies of partnership progress. The reports also typically require significant record-keeping. It helps--in preparing such reports--if materials are routinely retained that provide insights and information concerning partnership activities. An examination of Project STEP files reveals an array of statistical data, records of meetings, newspaper clippings, memos, copies of speeches and media interviews which were parts of the ongoing conduct of the project and its activities.

Brochures/Information Packages

These are basically for the purpose of external communication, but also can serve to reinforce the cohesiveness of partnership institutions. Project STEP's brochures have contained (1) a brief overview of project goals and objectives; (2) a description of the member institutions; (3) highlights of specific innovative programs; and (4) a brief description of the benefits of the partnership to its participants. The brochure also contains information about each participating institution and its involvement: the crest of each institution is represented; and each C.E.O. is pictured and is quoted regarding Project STEP and its impact. As is often the case in effective public relations and dissemination efforts, Project STEP staff maintain an extremely low profile, facilitating public recognition for the project among participating institutions.

Audiovisual Presentations

Project STEP has prepared and utilized several audiovisual presentations designed for meetings, conferences and the like. One particularly effective series of videotapes have been used to disseminate information concerning effective strategies for multicultural classrooms and for teachers of limited English proficient

(LEP) students. These videotapes have been used with students in the Teacher Education Program at UCI and in nearby colleges and universities and for training teacher educators statewide. The tapes not only provide contextual frameworks and expert practical demonstrations for prospective teachers but also have served to recognize the excellence and expertise of the bilingual instructional staff within the partner school district.

Conferences

Conference participation, including major addresses and panel presentations, are important ways in which specific institutional leaders can communicate to other educators about the partnership and its impacts. It is valuable to include representatives from both the K-12 and the postsecondary sectors in such conference presentations. Joint presentations by the Santa Ana Unified School District Superintendent and postsecondary administrators have been well-received and have had several positive effects on the STEP partnership itself. For example, the school district and postsecondary representatives have all seen demonstrable evidence of the significance of their serving as equal partners; second, representatives from each segment have gained a far greater understanding of the unique nature of Project STEP among state and federal educational reform efforts. In the case of Project STEP, joint presentations at conferences have shown educators throughout the region, state and nation the unusual value and success of a genuinely co-equal intersegmental partnership project.

Citations in Scholarly Publications

Project STEP has now been cited in several major scholarly publications, including ***Improving Science Education Through Local Alliances*** (1989) and ***A Crucial Agenda: Making Colleges and Universities Work Better for Minority Students*** (1989). Such citations serve to communicate the structure and dynamics of the program and to validate the importance of genuine intersegmental partnership as a model for others. Again, institutional leaders and initiatives reflecting both the K-12 and postsecondary sectors should be included in such publications where possible.

Adaptation Sites

A current Project STEP adaptation site is Compton Unified School District. The dissemination to and adaptation by the Compton School District in Los Angeles County has occurred through UCI's Early Outreach Program. Funding has been provided to adapt the elements of the STEP model, including the Administrative Council structure and selected services, to the needs of the Compton District. Continuing Carnegie support will permit work with Sherman Indian School. Both districts have large enrollments of underrepresented minority students, but the ethnic compositions of the districts vary markedly from the initial Project STEP sites. Compton Unified School District has a large enrollment of Black students and Sherman Indian School of Native American students, thereby providing the opportunity to structure program activities in accordance with the needs and priorities of these communities.

Membership in Collaborative Networks

Project STEP is a member of several collaborative networks, including the California Academic Partnership Program, the College Board's Educational EQuality Project and the Western Interstate Commission for Higher Education's multi-institutional structure. Membership within these networks has facilitated two-way communication with other partnerships and has provided an important source of enrichment and support.

Dissemination of a Casebook and Handbook

Documents such as this one are extremely valuable for both internal and external dissemination. Internally, they can be used in connection with staff development for new staff members, teachers and administrators. Externally, they provide models from which other partnerships can learn and build.

A Communications Checklist

- ❑ Have communication skills been considered in selecting Project Staff?
- ❑ Have communication strategies been discussed and shared among Project leaders?
- ❑ Is there a clear focus on information to be communicated and have appropriate communication vehicles been selected?

- ❑ Have meetings and project activities been structured to include meaningful participation from all members?
- ❑ Have inservice professional development activities been designed to include dialogues and seminars rather than primarily as expert presentations?
- ❑ Are representatives from both the K-12 and the postsecondary sectors invited to participate in and give collaborative presentations at conferences, state and federal educational reform programs, and the like?
- ❑ Have adaptation sites been identified which include other clusters of school districts and postsecondary institutions, including sites which may have somewhat different student populations?

- ❑ Has a project newsletter been developed for parents? for the educational community?
- ❑ Have resource guides, brochures, videotapes, and other communication vehicles been developed so that specific programs can be shared within and beyond the partnership?
- ❑ Have articles and monographs been undertaken and prepared collaboratively?
- ❑ Has a case history and handbook or similar document been prepared to share overall program goals and activities within and beyond the partnership?

CHAPTER 9

Sustaining Leadership and Momentum

Community education becomes not just schools opening up their facilities and extending their resources, but an ecosystem of institutions and agencies conscious of their responsibility for developing the knowledge, values, skills, and habits of a free people (John I. Goodlad 1984).

Six Essential Partnership Dynamics

- Open Communication
- Empowerment of Participants
- Development and Support of Partnership Culture
- Acknowledgement of the Long-Term Nature of Change
- Commitment of the Institutional Leaders
- Nourishment of Pride and Belonging

FOR most partnerships, the challenge of establishing a project is surpassed by the challenge of sustaining its momentum. Regardless of the attributes of the partnership, its goals, or the sophistication of its overall structure or member organization, a collaboration will not endure setbacks or nourish growth unless it has been able to inspire loyalty and commitment from its participants. From its inception a partnership must be sensitive to and cultivate the interpersonal and intersegmental dynamics that will sustain it over time. Several factors can impede or even destroy the momentum of a partnership project: changes in key personnel; insufficient communication about responsibilities; lack of access to resources or personnel; or just the natural relaxation of energy and focus that can occur as the partnership ages and grows.

leadership personnel at the school district level. In the process of experiencing and coping with challenges such as this, Project STEP has grown more resilient and productive. The source of the energy and strength of Project STEP's partnership lies largely in its appreciation for and sustaining of a critical set of interpersonal and intersegmental dynamics.

These dynamics will be discussed here in terms of:

- *what the interpersonal and intersegmental dynamics are as reflected in Project STEP;*
- *how such dynamics have been and can be achieved, based on the experience of Project STEP; and*
- *what positive effects they can have on a partnership.*

Open Communication

What does open communication mean?

> One of the most important concomitants of a school-university partnership may be the stimulation of dialogue, not only between school and university personnel as intended, but among educators within these institutions who are not ordinarily accustomed to engagement beyond the niceties of formal comunication (Sirotnik and Goodlad 1988, 217).

For some partnership participants, the ideas and information gained from intensive dialogue with a diverse group of educators is one of the main benefits of the partnership experience. The maintenance of a climate of open, deep and creative communication is essential to productive change: ideas are transmitted quickly; needs can be expressed and addressed relatively quickly; objectives, programs and resources can be redirected for greater effectiveness. Moreover, the creation of an infrastructure and atmosphere which provides sharing of information and perspectives and openness to suggestion, concerns and opinions helps to create and maintain greater commitment from individuals within the partnership.

How is open communication achieved?

Project STEP has incorporated into its organizational structure many avenues for communication to ensure that partners can discuss partnership goals and strategies productively. As much as possible, each partnership institution has a voice on all major decision-making committees. This process begins with the lead intersegmental entity, the Administrative Council, and is replicated throughout subcommittees and component task forces. Special subcommittees and site-level committees have also been composed of a range of participants from a particular institution to promote internal partnership member communication. For example, a Career/Guidance Committee has been composed of school district teachers, counselors, administrators and parents as well as representatives from other partnership institutions.

Beyond the organizational structure, partnership participants must feel secure operating at a level of open communication. As has been the case in Project STEP, an underlying tone of mutual respect and trust must be set from the inception of the partnership. Committee agendas should include significant amounts of time for dialogue, for communication about ongoing projects, for "good news" about initiatives, and for suggestions for improvements and for new directions. Staff members must be available to talk informally with representatives from partner institutions to respond to problems as they occur and to facilitate communication between institutions. Each participating school should have one or more facilitators, or coordinators, who can act as a liaison for others with the larger group. A newsletter, distributed to as many individual participants as possible, can recognize achievement, keep members and others in the participant institutions and communities informed, and serve as an avenue for further networking and sharing of ideas, as has been the experience of Project STEP.

What are the results of open communication?

Augenblick, Van de Water and Associates capture the productive effect that an environment of open communication has had on the Project STEP partnership. Its advantages have included sharing the opportunities open to and the expertise of individual partnership members:

> It was evident, at a STEP planning meeting, that each participant was extensively involved in other pursuits that brought them into contact with a wide range of people who might also be important to STEP success. They shared this information easily, almost casually, yet it was the kind of information that would open doors to needed expertise and fiscal resources. What I witnessed was a set of professionally committed and unusually active educators sharing their knowledge and experience in an atmosphere of trust and respect. Other factors, in addition to commitment, are necessary for success. I am convinced, however, that when strategically placed professionals combine commitment with an action orientation, the other factors will follow (Van de Water 1989, 20).

Empowerment of Participants

What does empowerment mean?

> Efforts at school improvement will not succeed without teacher leadership. In this country we have too long held teachers responsible for the condition of our schools without giving them responsibility--empowering them--to improve our schools (***Teaching in America: A Report of the Yale-New Haven Teachers Institute*** 1984, 8).

Current discussion of educational reform consistently emphasizes the beneficial effects of empowerment within the educational system. Literally meaning "giving power or authority," proponents of educational empowerment have argued that too many participants in the educational process have had too little participation in decision-making. The proponents argue that with empowerment, with the authority to make and influence decisions, will come greater commitment.

Project STEP has a fundamental belief in supporting the empowerment of its individual and institutional partners. At the institutional level, this means promoting opportunities for initiative as well as coequal participation between all the participating educational levels, so that the agenda and governance of the project are defined and shared equally between K-12 and postsecondary partners. Empowering participating individuals entails encouraging parents, teachers and students as well as administrators to take on leadership roles within the project. Project STEP's experiences have forcefully demonstrated the positive effects of an infrastructure and atmosphere that encourages both institutional and individual empowerment.

How is empowerment achieved?

For Project STEP, the principles of operation that have contributed the most to the empowerment and associated commitment of institutional and individual partners are shared participation and governance and coequal representation in decision-making. The principles of coequal participation and shared governance have stimulated individual commitment, particularly from K-12 and postsecondary faculty who have traditionally felt isolated from power within their own institutions. The Teacher Advisory Committee provides K-12 teachers with access to information and decision-making. Team-teaching cuts across disciplines and educational levels and reduces isolation. Faculty Forums, which are designed to stimulate discipline-specific and cross-disciplinary faculty exchanges and sharing of effective methodologies and resources, provide important enrichment and networking possibilities for faculty at all levels of the educational system. Coequal relationships between all levels of faculty and administration on Project Component Task Forces and Committees encourage a sense of shared educational purpose and contribution.

Participating institutions have coequal representation on all key committees from the Administrative Council to Component committees and task forces. This approach has stimulated substantial and continuing involvement from each institution in terms of commitment of resources and integration of the partnership into its long-term goals and objectives.

What are the results of empowerment?

These strategies aimed at fostering genuine teacher empowerment have had significant and positive effects on the partnership. The criticism often leveled against American schools is that, despite many eras of educational reform, very little has changed in the administration of schools and in the pedagogical approaches in the classroom. In order to bring about significant educational change, educators participating in Project STEP have adopted new methods and new relationships. The partnership has facilitated the emergence of new roles, based on an atmosphere of open communication and empowerment rarely possible in traditional educational settings. Leaders at the K-12 and postsecondary levels have recognized, legitimized and helped to preserve these new roles and relationships, thereby ensuring not only the momentum and dynamism of the partnership, but its very survival.

Administrative leaders must, as has been the case in Project STEP, be constantly alert to the fragility of the essential partnership elements of open communication, coequal participation and empowerment. No one institution or one set of administrative leaders can be allowed to dominate the partnership, no matter how well intentioned the motivation. Neither will the partnership achieve its potential if some of its member institutions are not genuinely committed to these fundamental principles. Education traditionally has been rooted in hierarchy across and within institutions, and participants can easily slip back into previous subordinate patterns which stifle creativity and commitment. Administrative leaders at both the K-12 and postsecondary level who are often responsible for the initial organization and focus of the partnership, must be prepared to gradually relinquish much of their control over power and leadership as the individual participants take on a greater role. As the partnership develops and expands, administrators must remain sensitive to sharing power and to preserving dialogue as a means to decision-making. Only in such a supportive atmosphere will partnership leaders and participants particularly at the school-site maintain the level of proactive commitment and innovation necessary for educational reform.

The Development of a Partnership Culture

What is a Partnership Culture?

> A major reason for promoting partnerships that include at least one university is that schools (or school districts) and universities differ not in degree but in kind. They differ in purpose, function, structure, clienele, reward systems, rules and regulations, ambience, ethos; schools and universities are markedly different cultural entities. Herein lie both the promise of a productive school-university partnership and the sandtraps, swamps, and quicksands standing in the way of a successful marriage (Sirotnik and Goodlad 1988, 14).

An extremely influential factor in Project STEP's ongoing success as a partnership project is its emergence as a separate identity or culture to the partner institutions. Educational institutions traditionally maintain well-defined structures of hierarchy, communication, and distinctive organizational goals. With a partnership project, however, participants need to be encouraged to accept an added set of goals, procedures and relationships different from those of their separate institutions. Priorities shift from individual to collaborative means and ends. The processes of decision-making reflect a completely different perspective. Far more than typically is possible within a given educational institution, a partnership can develop norms and behaviors fostering trust, egalitarianism, and organizational creativity.

The functioning of a partnership as a separate culture, with its own norms, language and behaviors, can ultimately produce more significant and lasting educational change than any individual initiative or program component. The separate partnership culture allows participants to explore approaches and methodologies that the individual institutions might not otherwise even consider. Ideally, partner institutions will ultimately adopt some of the cooperative and egalitarian norms and behaviors for themselves, thereby enabling the partnership culture to enrich their own functioning while also creating an environment conducive to broadening involvement in it.

How is a partnership culture achieved?

Project STEP has achieved a partnership culture by ensuring that every aspect of its administrative and pedagogical approach is infused with certain fundamental values: shared governance, open communication and coequal representation. Partners have felt secure with these important "cultural" norms primarily because the chief executive officers have genuinely endorsed the partnership principles and because the norms have repeatedly proven successful as a means to achieving specific institutional goals.

What effect does a partnership culture have?

In Project STEP, the existence of a strong culture separate from those of the individual participating institutions has had several important effects. First, partnership members are secure to face problems and communicate concerns about their own institutions, knowing that the partnership culture is designed to remediate these problems.

For example, both the K-12 and postsecondary partners can face such specific concerns as low numbers of minority students continuing to higher education. Santa Ana Unified School District (SAUSD), the University of California, Irvine, California State University, Fullerton and Rancho Santiago College began their involvement with Project STEP with the realization that only 10% of Santa Ana students pursued a postsecondary education.

In addressing an issue such as this, postsecondary institutions can deal with such concerns as their distance from the reality of the K-12 environment from which their students emerge. This is a particularly relevant concern of schools of education, whose faculty may not be sufficiently equipped to prepare future teachers for the reality of multicultural classrooms, including many limited-English speaking students. In fact, the UCI Office of Teacher Education has benefitted significantly from the expertise of outstanding bilingual educators within the Santa Ana Unified School District. Videotaped demonstration lessons by selected ESL teachers from the district are now shown to all teacher education candidates, illustrating successful instructional strategies for culturally and linguistically diverse classrooms. An unanticipated benefit has been a large increase in the number of new teachers trained in the university's selective teacher credentialing program seeking and obtaining teaching positions within the Santa Ana Unified School District--a rapidly growing district in need of new teachers who have been thoroughly exposed to issues and methodologies of second language learning as part of their teacher preparation.

A partnership also provides a strong support structure for the "risk-takers" who are inclined to initiate and carry through with needed educational changes. One principal in the Santa Ana Unified School District has, for example, established heterogeneous grouping throughout the school for which the principal is responsible. Few principals in other urban school districts attempt to practice heterogeneous grouping despite increasingly positive evaluations in educational research. The STEP partnership has provided the environment to enable the principal to take this risk and to build upon the principal's initiative in expanding the use of heterogeneous grouping districtwide.

The partnership culture also serves to promote sharing and adoption of specific norms and behaviors among partner members. For example, peer tutoring is a fairly standard support service provided by the postsecondary institutions. It is rare to find established peer tutoring programs in K-12 schools within urban areas. Utilizing the services of the Rancho Santiago Community College Learning Center, Project STEP initiated a peer tutoring program within the SAUSD that has now become recognized by district principals as integral to the achievement of their curricular goals.

Acknowledgement of the Long-Term Nature of Change

Why must educational change be viewed as long-term?

The National Commission on the Humanities is among those groups that has demonstrated an understanding of the fact that lasting and meaningful educational change does not come about quickly and that partnerships can be critical tools in such change processes:

> Because schools change slowly, we endorse models of school-college collaboration that emphasize long-term cooperation (*Teaching in America: A Report of the Yale-New Haven Teachers Institute,* 1984, 8).

John Goodlad warns potential partnerships that "the enemy of renewal is the quick-fix" (Sirotnik and Goodlad 1988). He goes on to note that:

> The ultimate indicators of the success of a school-university partnership are not what gets marked up on the scoreboard, however important short-term accomplishments are as motivators. The nature and quality of institutional and individual renewal serve as the source for determining evaluative indicators (Sirotnik and Goodlad 1988, 224).

Many partnerships fail because the impact is fleeting; it cannot be sustained beyond a particular funding source. Others fail because their impact is too slight, too tangential to the curricular goals of the district. It is not surprising that K-12 or postsecondary educators are often skeptical that intersegmental involvement in their activities will support rather than impede their goals. A partnership must acknowledge from its inception that the results of significant educational changes--including those involving intersegmental collaboration-- do not come about quickly.

How can acceptance of the long-term nature of change be achieved?

Much of STEP's success in institutionalizing curricular and organizational changes has resulted from the project's commitment to a long-term collaborative process. It has included planning, research and development, inservice, training, implementation, evaluation of both processes and outcomes, and subsequent further refinement of the project components.

Although this long-term collaborative process may seem less efficient than more autocratic decision-making and implementation, it has significant benefits for a partnership--first, participants have more time to reflect collectively on appropriate curricular and organizational direction; second, there is room in this process for fostering the kind of flux, adaptation and transformation that institutions such as schools rarely promote; third, participants feel more ownership of and commitment to decisions and goals that emerge from the collaborative process; and fourth, the understanding that the process will feature ongoing evaluation and revision stimulates creativity and risk-taking in the critical early stages of program development.

What effect does it have when partners accept a long-term approach to change?

At a practical level, a planning and implementation process which accepts change as a long-term process leads to sustained institutional change. A case in point relates to a number of Project STEP objectives which were aligned with the long-range plans of the Santa Ana Unified School District for implementing curricular reform consistent with the six-year cycle utilized by the State Department of Education. Attention to a new State curriculum and a District implementation plan for each discipline has been sustained long enough to assure that the State curriculum and textbooks adoption results in important instructional changes within the District. For example, beginning with a review of the current curriculum in 1985, Mathematics curriculum revisions were made by the joint secondary/postsecondary STEP Mathematics Component committee in light of the new ***California Mathematics Framework*** and ***Model Curriculum Standards.*** In the implementation phase for the next two years, joint staff development will be provided to identify, demonstrate and encourage teaching strategies to complement and carry out curricular revisions. Refinements in the curriculum and an evaluation of the entire process have now led to the review and revision of mathematics assessment practices in the district.

Commitment of the Institutional Leaders to Partnership Goals

What level of commitment is needed from institutional leaders?

The commitment of dynamic and positive leaders from the participant educational institutions is essential to the long-term success of the partnership. These leaders must inspire other participants by their faith in and support for the partnership; they can help the partnership withstand crises and frustrations; they have enormous influence over personnel and resources within their institutions; and they usually belong to a network of institutions and individuals who can lend further support from the outside.

How can commitment from institutional leaders be achieved?

From Project STEP's experience, there appear to be three stages of leadership commitment that need to be achieved by the partnership and that need to occur among one or more leaders from each participant institution.

STAGE 1

What will the partnership do for me as an institutional leader . . . and for us institutionally?

As individuals, institutional leaders should gain benefits of empowerment, communication and information and access to positive rewards and to resources that the partnership provides. Empowerment for institutional leaders comes in such forms as directing the institution's participation in the partnership and selecting institutional members for participation on key decision-making and implementation committees and task forces. For example, in Project STEP, CEO's have selected their own representatives for the Administrative Council and have helped to shape project components carried out under their institution's leadership. Commitment on the part of institutional leaders is also enhanced by their being kept informed of and being able to contribute to the overall framework for all key meetings and activities, major reports, proposals for external funding, and the like. The commitment of leaders to the partnership is further strengthened by giving individual recognition for their involvement: their role should be recognized in partnership publications; they should contribute to press releases and interviews; and they should attend national conferences and forums as representatives and spokespersons of the partnership.

Project STEP has always recognized the contribution of its institutional leaders, particularly the school district leader, whose commitment to the project is especially critical. The current Santa Ana School District Superintendent, Dr. Rudy Castruita, has enabled the partnership to grow and thrive in numerous pioneering directions. He has been uniquely able to represent the partnership and describe its dynamics from the perspective of a school district superintendent at the annual conference of the American Association of Higher Education and for research conducted by the Western Interstate Commission for Higher Education, including its report: ***A Crucial Agenda: Making Colleges and Universities Work Better for Minority Students.***

Institutional leaders will continue to support a partnership if they perceive it as a means to achieving valued ends--an alliance with other institutions and resources that assist them to realize some of their immediate and long-term institutional goals. Project STEP has always been responsive to the institutional needs and goals of its participant members. For example, changes in student enrollment and teacher demographics indicated in 1987 that Santa Ana Unified School District required recruitment of approximately 400 new teachers within two years. In response to the Superintendent's request, Project STEP assisted the Assistant Superintendent for Personnel, the supervisor of instructional assistants, and the Director of Bilingual Education in the design and implementation of a comprehensive strategy aimed at helping experienced bilingual instructional assistants to become credentialed classroom teachers. A districtwide conference was held for instructional aides, entitled "Instructional Strategies and Career Ladder Opportunities." The District Superintendent provided the keynote address for the 450 instructional aides who attended this inservice, encouraging them to acquire further training from the partnership institutions in order to become teachers within the district. Representatives from each postsecondary institution described the programs and resources available to assist them in becoming classroom teachers and established customized procedures to facilitate their taking advantage of these opportunities.

In ***Improving Science Education Through Local Alliances,*** the Chancellor of UC Irvine, described how Project STEP served an important institutional need of the University:

> [In view of the current demographics], I can't imagine a more important issue at a public California university than getting more minority students. We must deliver the university to the next century--and make sure it's still a university (Atkin and Atkin 1989, 63).

STAGE 2

What can we do as partnership institutions for each other?

Gradually, if the partnership can demonstrate success in satisfying individual institutional goals, the leaders can begin to perceive the partnership as playing an increasingly important part in the realization of long-term, inter-institutional and intersegmental goals.

For example, the K-12 and postsecondary partners in Project STEP have worked together to coordinate evaluation and accountability reports of high schools, looking at strengths and weaknesses in individual schools. This process enables the K-12 sector to better prepare students for college and universities. It allows postsecondary representatives to identify ways in which their faculty can participate in this process. In the previous example of helping K-12 bilingual instructional classroom aides become classroom teachers and exposing them to course offerings and financial support available at the postsecondary level, the postsecondary sector gained well-qualified teacher education candidates in the vitally important area of bilingual education.

STAGE 3

What can we do as an institution for the partnership?

Institutional leaders will begin to internalize the values of the partnership and to actively promote them when the partnership proves its success in satisfying individual and intersegmental goals. If the partnership gains legitimacy and visibility with the State or even at the federal level, the commitment of the institutional leaders is likely to be even greater.

Project STEP has been very successful in satisfying institutional needs. It has been extremely fortunate to have the support of institutional leaders who are committed to collaboration. Chancellor Jack Peltason of the University of California, Irvine, has, for example, been an ardent believer in the benefits of inter-institutional cooperation throughout his career as a postsecondary leader. Dr. Jewel Cobb, President of California State University, Fullerton, has contributed yearly to the partnership budget. Dr. Robert Jensen, Chancellor of Rancho Santiago College, has supported the partnership and the tutorial component of Project STEP by donating fiscal support annually. Dr. Rudy Castruita, Superintendent of Santa Ana Unified School District, has contributed his direct personal leadership to the project by serving as Co-Director.

What effect does the commitment of institutional leaders have on a partnership?

If the partnership can develop and sustain the commitment of institutional leaders, and through them the commitment of entire institutions, the stage is set for extraordinary educational reform opportunities. Once typically isolated institutions open themselves to each other and begin to share resources and expertise, they are able to achieve progress at a rate that would be impossible alone.

For postsecondary institutions, new opportunities arise for practice-based research and development initiatives in a variety of disciplines and K-12 curriculum areas. Unquestionably, Departments or Schools of Education gain enormously from the opportunities to improve the preparation of teachers through cooperative arrangements. However, it is particularly important to note that other departments also gain substantially, not only by bridging the gap between the K-12 and postsecondary levels, with resultant improvements in the preparation of college bound students, but also through collaborative research and school-based disciplinary and cross-disciplinary inquiring involving K-12 educators.

For the K-12 sector, commitment to the partnership brings access to human, institutional and financial resources development of innovative ideas and activities. Professional isolation for the K-12 educator is reduced. Further, new possibilities emerge for students within the partnership school district, who can now be engaged in a continuum of educational opportunities and activities involving a range of postsecondary institutions.

Nourishment of Pride and Belonging

How important is a sense of pride and belonging?

Participants in a partnership project are by definition involved in a venture that will cause them extra work and require a commitment of time and energy. It is not sufficient to emphasize the practical benefits that will accrue from their participation for the collaboration to be a valued activity. Participants must feel proud to belong to the partnership, particularly seeing the benefits to the students and teachers who are most impacted by the program. Project STEP has worked hard to design an environment of pride associated with belonging to a valued effort, capturing and drawing upon the desire to make socially valuable contributions characteristic of most who choose education as a profession.

How is a sense of pride and belonging achieved?

Pride and commitment are typically engendered in similar ways for most participants in a partnership. First, leaders--such as task force leaders, special project leaders and committee members--must be given ownership for the programs that they have developed. They must be allowed significant control in developing and carrying out these programs and they must be recognized for the work they have done. At Administrative Council meetings, participants should be invited to give updates on projects and share successes. Newsletters distributed throughout the partnership should communicate the contributions of specific individuals and teams to the entire partnership. These successes may be large or small, but their recognition by the partnership leadership is extremely important.

Second, the partnership must demonstrate its recognition of valuable roles played by its "foot soldiers,"--individuals such as instructors and counselors who are directly interfacing with students and parents. These individuals must be allowed the opportunity to take on leadership roles and to share their experiences and expertise with peers and other partnership participants in situations like intersegmental Faculty Forums. They must also be individually recognized, as other Project STEP participants are, in major reports. Instructors at the K-12 level work in a utilitarian environment; few school funds are spent on providing small luxuries for them, such as comfortable lounges, private office space or special dinners. The partnership can also recognize the contributions of those on the "front lines" by taking steps that demonstrate appreciation for their valuable effort: stipends for extra responsibilities; release time for conferences; comfortable settings for their work; and the hosting of meetings which bestow dignity through the social graces often reserved for the more traditionally recognized "special" guests.

Students, who are, after all, the end goal of any educational partnership, must also be instilled with a sense of pride and uniqueness if they are to exert themselves to achieve the levels expected of them. In the Project STEP Partnership, students are rewarded in a variety of ways. These have included their being recognized as cross-age or peer tutors; their being invited to participate at postsecondary institutions for special events and programs; their being paid to assist in project activities; and their receiving awards recognizing their valuable contributions.

A Checklist for Sustaining Leadership and Momentum

- ❑ Have avenues for achieving open communication been developed in the partnership?
- ❑ Have strategies been adopted to ensure empowerment of participants, including teachers, counselors, parents and students?
- ❑ Are partnership principles emphasized, communicated and demonstrated, so that all participants understand them and the degree to which they are valued?
- ❑ Is the partnership addressing some of the immediate, short-term goals of participant institutions?
- ❑ Are partnership goals aligned to the long range goals of the participant school district and postsecondary institutions?
- ❑ Are institutional leaders supported in and rewarded for their commitment?
  - ❑ Are they kept well-informed?
  - ❑ Are secondary and postsecondary leaders treated coequally? at conferences? in publications?
  - ❑ Does publicity about the partnership cite them?
- ❑ Has the partnership been structured to give task forces and committees ownership for the programs they develop?

- ☐ Have strategies been incorporated into the partnership for motivating and sustaining individual contributions--including recognizing and rewarding hard work and achievements?

    - ☐ Are facilitators, coordinators and participants given stipends for extra responsibilities?
    - ☐ Are monies set aside for release time, for special conferences, for unique privileges and opportunities, for meetings which recognize and celebrate the roles of the "foot soldiers"?
    - ☐ Are participating students given recognition, postsecondary opportunities, or otherwise made to feel "special"?

Afterword

All segments of the society now agree that our educational system needs radical change if we are to meet the economic challenges of the future. The evidence--both statistical and anecdotal--clearly indicates that our international economic position is slipping, and that a strong link exists between this slippage and the quality of education. However, we must also openly acknowledge that there is another reason that our system of education requires radical change. Simply put, we have a moral obligation to ensure that all citizens--regardless of race, sex, religion, culture and age--are afforded strong and equal educational opportunities. We must have the highest level of concern about this situation, not only for economic reasons, but because equal educational opportunities are an absolutely critical component of a just and egalitarian society. Our ideals, as well as our gross national product, are at stake. The combination of these two imperatives dictates the kinds of solutions that are acceptable.

If we are to meet both the moral and economic challenges that face us, a mediocre education for the many is as unacceptable as a quality education for the few. Acceptable solutions recognize and acknowledge that quality and equality are tightly interwoven and one cannot exist without the other. Acceptable solutions require an approach to education that is built on the assumption that everyone can do quality academic work. Acceptable solutions are designed to enhance student performance and to raise the level of expectations of students, parents, teachers and everyone else involved in the educational process. The assumption that all students have ability, not tacit expectations of their inability, must serve as the foundation for building a new system for teaching all young people. It is an ideal which can be realized.

The recent consensus on the need for educational reform is best illustrated by the highly publicized efforts of the federal and state governments to define national goals and set a subsequent course of action. Their joining the discussion adds urgency to the call that has already been sounded by educators, business and community leaders and those in the social services. The door to change is now more open than it has been in the recent past. However, we do not know how long the national interest will remain at its current high level and, therefore, we must act quickly to capitalize on the opportunities that present themselves to us.

The wide acceptance of the need for educational reform has been accompanied by a shift away from defining the problems to defining and implementing solutions. With the educational reform movement over a decade old, many problems have already been identified and analyzed, providing a base on which action programs have been designed and put into effect. Many of these programs have borne results, giving us all a substantial body of knowledge on what is needed to improve education and where effective remedies lie.

The very significant work accomplished in the area of improving education has come from a wide variety of sectors. These include schools, school districts, institutions of higher learning, various levels of government, foundations, education associations, community groups and social service agencies. This is as it should be. All hold part of the answer to a complex puzzle and each must play an active role in creating the final design. To use the words of another author,

> schooling may be organized into discrete categories for administrative purposes, but education is a long-term process without such artificial boundaries. Students' experiences at any level of schooling necessarily will affect subsequent experiences and subsequent school possibilities. Problems at one level have consequences for all levels that follow (Sosniak 1989, 3).

It is not an exaggeration to say that without collaborative efforts, we will be unable to put together fully that system (or systems) needed to meet the ongoing, complex and critical needs of students.

Much of the pioneering work in this area has been conducted in the school-to-college arena. This arena represents a critical linkage point between powerful sectors of our education system. Without the ability of an increasingly large number of secondary school students to succeed in this specific transition from high school to college, it will be impossible for this nation to have an educational system that achieves its potential. Our task is to examine those collaborative programs that have succeeded so that they can be replicated.

The College Board has been proud to play a role in this effort. In 1983, the Board, through the Educational EQuality Project, began to develop a network of model programs for school-college collaboratives focusing on academic equity for all students. Initially, thirteen prgrams were brought together in this effort. Over a seven year period, they and other school-college collaboratives that joined the network have worked together to share information and ideas, give and get technical assistance, develop publications and provide advice on College Board activities. Project STEP has been involved in this effort since its inception.

Diversification is already a reality in Santa Ana schools. With a student population of 89% of whom are Hispanic and 56% of whom are of limited English speaking proficiency, Santa Ana is today what educators project the "school district of the future" will be. However, the ethnic diversity alone is not what distinguishes this school district. What really distinguishes Santa Ana is its conviction that diversity is a strength, not a handicap; that diversity contributes to the development of a rich cultural basis for educating all students. Santa Ana has cast aside the special programs of the 1960s in favor of a comprehensive system that views each of its students and his/her background as something to be nurtured and treasured, not split up or homogenized. It absolutely accepts the idea that quality and equality can and must co-exist.

As one reviews the work of Project STEP, several critical factors that explain the project's success can be identified. First, members of the collaborative have been oriented to action. Change in practice and attitude has been embraced, not rejected. Second, Project STEP has been a broad-based movement that has continued to grow from serving 1400 students a year in 1984-85 to 3000 students in 1989-90. During this time, faculty and staff participation along with parent involvement has remained strong at over 300 and 400 respectively. Third, Project STEP has actively sought input from every institution and every person. It has been a democratic process through which all contribute and all learn. As a result, the end product has been better students and better education.

There is much to be learned from this effort both in terms of process and ideals. Project STEP and others have understood that the process could only be determined once the ideals were clearly defined. The emphasis on quality and equality has driven their work and it must also be the driving force in our work as we continue to reshape American education. Neither ideal can be sacrificed if we are to succeed in meeting our obligations as educators and as citizens.

A primary function of the College Board is to further both quality and equality. This has become our single greatest priority and, in March 1989, the Trustees of the College Board adopted an equity goal for the remainder of the twentieth century. It states that:

> . . . by the end of the twentieth century, individuals from traditionally underrepresented groups will have access to and complete two-year and four-year college education at the same rate as traditional students.

This goal is an ambitious one but one that deserves our attention. We will be actively pursuing efforts--through our core programs, the Educational EQuality Project, demonstration programs and national advocacy--to ensure that we draw closer to the goal. Collaborative efforts, such as those exemplified by Project STEP, will continue to be part of what we believe is the answer to the critical problems facing education.

Donald M. Stewart
President
The College Board
April, 1990

APPENDICES

APPENDIX A

A Chronology of Project STEP

This chronology is categorized into four phases that emphasize the ongoing evolution of the STEP structure, programs and concepts of K-12/ postsecondary partnership:

- The Early Development of the STEP Concept: 1975-- Background and Enabling Conditions

- The "UCI/SAUSD" STEP Project: 1983-- A Member of The College Board's Educational EQuality Project Models Program for School-College Collaboration

- Project STEP: "A Model of Intersegmental Collaboration:" 1985--. A California Academic Partnership Program (CAPP) Project

- Project STEP: "A Partnership for the Advancement of Learning:" 1987--Present. CAPP Showcase and Carnegie Corporation of New York Support

Throughout this chronology, many of the people who have contributed to the development and implementation of Project STEP activities are noted. The STEP Administrative Council and Components structure were established in July 1984 and January 1985 respectively; rosters for Council members and Component coordinators are provided within the subsequent sections.

Since the 1984-1985 academic year, twice as many students have been directly involved in project activities each year, and three times as many faculty and staff from the STEP partner institutions have been engaged, for an annual total of over 2,800 students and over 300 faculty, administrators, counselors, and staff.

The Early Development of the STEP Concept: 1975 - 1983

Project STEP represents the coalescence of a history of efforts between UC Irvine and the Santa Ana Unified School District (SAUSD) that began with initiation of the University of California Early Outreach Partnership Program in 1975. At UCI, this program was implemented to work in the local Santa Ana intermediate schools and other districts to motivate and prepare students from ethnic minority groups under-represented at the university to enroll in college preparatory courses required for admission to the University of California. These courses are known in the UC system as the "A-F" required courses.

The program expanded to include the high schools in 1978 in order to follow up on the students' progress and assist student preparation in critical academic skills. The primary program strategy was to train university students and place them in the schools to provide motivational and academic services. This period also marked the beginning of efforts to inform and involve parents.

In 1980 the intermediate and high school programs were combined at UCI to form the current structure of the Early Outreach Partnership Program under the aegis of the Educational Opportunity Program/Student Affirmative Action Office (EOP/SAA). One of the first outcomes of the restructuring was the development of the "pipeline concept" that created the following sequential development of services for students as they proceeded through the Partnership Program: at the intermediate level, motivation and information; at the ninth, tenth and eleventh grade, academic support and development; at the twelfth grade, assistance with the college application process.

Meetings and discussions were held between UCI and SAUSD officials to determine how to adapt existing activities and foster new ones to meet the challenge of improving student academic preparation. These meetings were the genesis for the eventual development of the STEP concept, the "Student/Teacher Education Project," which represented a dual focus on the students and the teachers of the Santa Ana district.

Two parallel events were occurring, one at SAUSD and the other at UCI, that would eventually create the conditions for a successful collaboration. In Superintendent Harrison's letter of support for the

STEP concept written to Chancellor Aldrich in August 1981, he explained:

> As Superintendent of the Santa Ana Unified School District, I have been searching for ways to ". . . increase student skills and aspirations and to provide secondary school personnel with resources necessary to strengthen A-F course curriculum." To use a term common to our students, this proposal is "right on."
>
> The link between the university and the high school that STEP forges will give everyone the strength and vision to improve post-secondary educational opportunities for our students. Like our students, the teachers, too, need to know that someone cares and believes in them. That restoration in their faith and confidence will affect the attitude of every student they touch.

At UCI, EOP/SAA staff were meeting with UCI faculty and discussing ideas to improve the level of preparation of incoming freshman students. One major conclusion reached as a result of these meetings was a recognition of the need for stronger articulation and dialogue between secondary school faculty and University faculty.

Subsequently, a series of discussions took place between UCI staff, high school principals and district officials which led to a planned series of forums between university and secondary school faculty to discuss the problems of student academic preparation. The forums were organized with the intention of developing an action plan designed to implement collaborative efforts that would improve academic achievement.

The Vice Chancellor, William Lillyman, in an address to the Student Preparation Meeting at the UC Office of the President--Universitywide on December 19, 1983, provided a history of these events and the UCI campus-wide response to the issues of under-preparation:

> When we began to examine the problems, it became clear that we would make no significant progress if we did everything piecemeal . . . These administrative changes, it should be made very clear, would not of themselves necessarily have produced unified action. They do have at least the function of clearing away obstacles, and they provide opportunities.
>
> UCI was fortunate in having both staff and faculty with the ability to understand that we all wanted the same thing, or something close to the same thing. I am particularly glad to note that the goals and aims of Student Affirmative Action were recognized as being part and parcel of the goals of Radius [a committee appointed by Lillyman to coordinate UCI's curricular outreach efforts]. We are especially concerned with the preparation of students for the University; but we know that this preparation cannot be accomplished unless the schools achieve overall improvements. In short, those specifically concerned with Student Affirmative Action and those specifically concerned with the improvement of curriculum and instruction are absolutely tied together. UCI came to realize this as an institution during 1982-1983. (Lillyman 1983.)

Major initiatives were occurring at the system-wide levels of administration for all of the "segments" of public education in California: the State Department of Education (SDE); the California Community Colleges (CCC); the California State University (CSU); and the University of California. In January 1983, the first "Intersegmental" dinner was hosted by the UC Office of the President for the Los Angeles Community College District (LACCD), designed by a planning committee comprised of policy level representatives from each of the segments. This workshop produced a plan for a series of "intersegmental" conferences involving the LACCD and local southern California campuses of the CSU and UC segments.

In attendance at the May 1983 first conference in this series hosted at Los Angeles Harbor College, Manuel Gomez volunteered to host the second conference in the series at UCI in October 1983. Also in October 1983, he made a commitment to "inter-segmental collaboration" in his testimony at hearings sponsored by Teresa Hughes on proposed legislation to establish the California Academic Partnership Program (CAPP), which would create a funding agency to foster school/college collaborations engaged in curriculum enhancement, staff development, and student support services to increase the enrollment of ethnic minority students in postsecondary education.

The "UCI/SAUSD STEP Project:" 1983 - 1984

• **February 1983--Seed Grant from the University of California Office of the President for STEP.** A seed grant of $8,000 was received by STEP originators for development of the concept of academic collaboration through a series of Faculty Forums.

• **April 1983--Forum on Academic Preparation: Beginning the Dialogue.** Representatives from the Santa Ana Unified School District met with UCI representatives to share their respective views and experiences related to under-preparation issues. SAUSD representatives included Superintendent John Dunworth and district level administrators, principals and assistant principals as well as counselors from the high schools and the intermediate schools. Academic personnel included department chairs and faculty in the areas of science, mathematics, foreign language, fine arts, social sciences and English. UCI representatives included The Vice Chancellor William Lillyman and his staff, EOP/SAA staff, various UCI deans, and faculty from chemistry, fine arts, writing, humanities, physical sciences, foreign language, biological sciences, physics and mathematics.

The UCI perspective was presented by William Lillyman, The Vice Chancellor; Manuel Gomez, Director of EOP/SAA--Outreach; and Rita Peterson, Director of the Office of Teacher Education. The SAUSD perspective was presented by Ralph Jack, Assistant Superintendent,

Vergil Hettick, Director of Secondary Curriculum, and the three SAUSD high school principals: Gerald Arriola, Santa Ana High School; Ed Krass, Saddleback High School; and Ivan McKinney, Valley High School.

Two successful models of college preparation in the secondary schools were presented, the College Core Curriculum project from Banning High School in Wilmington and College Prep Program from Huntington Park High School. Mare Taagepera, Director of the UCI Summer Science Institute, and John Hollowell, UCI Director of Writing and Co-Director with Carol Booth Olson of the UCI California Writing Project, provided descriptions of their curricular outreach programs.

In the afternoon, faculty from UCI met with the teachers from the secondary schools in their respective disciplines for open discussion. The responses to an evaluation form completed by the participants indicated a high level of enthusiasm on the part of university and secondary school faculty to continue with the collaboration and to proceed to the next stage of development, which was to create an action plan. The evaluation also indicated that the faculty discussions by disciplines were valuable and should continue.

- **May 1983--From Dialogue to Action Plans**

Forum on Academic Preparation: School Plans. Between the first and second forums, UCI Early Outreach Partnership staff met with school site administrators to assist in the development of plans to initiate the collaborative for each school. Participants from the previous conference returned to this second forum to hear and discuss the school plans.

Carl Hartman, UCI Associate Vice Chancellor for Academic Affairs, and Ralph Jack, SAUSD Assistant Superintendent, provided introductory remarks and introduced representatives for university-based resources including Hilda Solis, Coordinator of Cal-SOAP, Antonio De Castro, Coordinator of Early Outreach Partnership, and Jim Dunning, Director of Admissions. Vergil Hettick, SAUSD Director of Secondary Curriculum, moderated a panel of high school assistant principals who presented comprehensive school plans. The plans included student identification and recognition, objectives for counseling, teacher enhancement and recognition, parent and community involvement, university involvement, and curricular review activities.

Santa Ana High School's plan, for example, established an educational program called "PREP: A Pathway to College." Eight common elements within these school plans were identified and presented by the SAUSD as "The College Core Curriculum."

During the afternoon session, UCI faculty members met with their secondary school counterparts to continue their discussions initiated at the first forum. A consensus was reached to continue the discipline-based discussions on an ongoing basis and plans were made to arrange for faculty exchanges between UCI and SAUSD for the development of curricular review and enhancement mechanisms.

Joint Visitation to Willard Intermediate School by UCI and Santa Ana High School Project STEP Representatives. Counselors from Santa Ana High and UCI Early Outreach Partnership staff made classroom presentations of the "PREP" program to all eighth grade students at Willard Intermediate School. Based on student interest in pursuing college plans, fifty percent of the ninth grade students were designated as college preparatory students.

Spanish for Spanish Speakers Class. A review by UCI Early Outreach Partnership staff revealed that students taking a "Spanish for Spanish Speakers" class in Santa Ana schools were not receiving credit towards completion of the foreign language requirement for UC admissions. A letter was sent by the SAUSD to UC Systemwide to correct the oversight. As a result, students were given retroactive credit for the class and the class is now designated as college preparatory.

- **June 1983--Supporting the Agenda: Review, Reflection and Resource Coordination**

Meeting of SAUSD High School Principals with UCI Representatives. The three high school principals met with UCI representatives to assess the progress of the project. The major items discussed were the determination of a timeline and appropriate methods to continue successful implementation.

A Visit by the State Department of Education. Representatives of the Special Projects Division of the State Department of Education (SDE) met with UCI and SAUSD representatives to learn about Project STEP. SDE representatives indicated a particular interest in learning about the "enabling conditions" that permitted the development of this successful effort. They also expressed a desire to be kept informed of future developments.

UCI Project Radius Plan. The Radius Committee was established by direction of The Vice Chancellor William Lillyman. Under the aegis of the UCI Office of Teacher Education, it was initiated in November 1982 as a committee responsible for development of a plan for coordination of UCI curricular outreach activities related to secondary schools. In June 1983, this plan was released. At this time the committee included the UCI directors of Project STEP, the Summer Science Institute, the California Writing Project, the California Math Project, the National Science Foundation Mentor Teacher Project, and the National Endowment for the Humanities Mentor Teacher Program.

- **Summer 1983--The Summer Institutes**

UCI California Writing Project Summer Institute. Twelve teachers from the SAUSD were sponsored through UCI Office of Academic Affairs Student Affirmative Action (SAA) funding to participate in this summer institute, selected on the basis of their interest in sharing the instructional strategies with fellow teachers. A pilot English class incorporating Writing Project approaches had been developed and discussions were underway for implementation of this project in the SAUSD.

UCI Summer Science Institute. Teachers from the SAUSD were selected to participate in the UCI Summer Science Institute for secondary school teachers. This six-week program was designed by Mare Taagepera and George Miller of the UCI Department of Chemistry to enhance the teaching of science in the secondary schools.

Summer Residential Program Funded by the National Endowment for the Humanities. Approximately 120 Santa Ana Unified School District students were selected to participate in a special ten-day residential program on the UCI campus conducted by the Early Outreach

Partnership Program. The program activities were designed to develop an increased understanding of the humanities through a participatory learning experience.

Junior High School Summer Program. Approximately 120 junior high school students from several school districts including the SAUSD participated in a three-day residential program designed by Early Outreach staff for exposure to the University environment, information on preparation for high school, and assistance in developing critical study skills.

- **August 1983--A Visit by the College Board.** Aaron Fink, Senior Advisor to The College Board's Educational EQuality Project Models Program for School/College Collaboration, met with UCI and SAUSD representatives to describe Project EQuality. He expressed interest in including STEP in this nationwide network of school-college collaborations organized under the aegis of The College Board.

- **September 1983--School Starts with STEP**

STEP Invited to Join Project EQuality. Project STEP was invited to become a member of the College Board's Educational EQuality Project Models Program for School-College Collaboration.

UCI Faculty Participate in SAUSD Teacher Orientation Sessions. SAUSD annually plans a week of orientation prior to the beginning of classroom instruction. UCI faculty were invited by the district to join SAUSD faculty during these orientation inservice sessions in their respective disciplines. The invitation by the district for UCI faculty to join these sessions was later credited for encouraging many further activities.

STEP Students and Mentor Teachers at Santa Ana High School. Twenty-one teachers from across the disciplines at Santa Ana High School volunteered to serve as mentors for STEP students. Mentor responsibilities included counseling, tutoring, and monitoring the academic progress of students assigned to them. The students were identified by Santa Ana High School counselors and Early Outreach

Partnership Program staff as having the desire to pursue a post-secondary education.

UCI Tutors. University students were hired through the Early Outreach Partnership Program to serve as tutors and counselors to work in the SAUSD high schools. The student tutors were matched with mentor teachers to serve STEP students.

Group Study Workshop. Uri Triesman, from UC Berkeley's Professional Development Program, presented a workshop at Santa Ana High School on forming study groups. In attendance were the mentor teachers and university student tutors. The purpose of the workshop was to learn various techniques to encourage high school students to form study groups.

- **October 1983--Testimony at Hearing of the Assembly Committee on Education Chaired by Teresa Hughes.** Manuel Gomez was invited to provide a statement in support of Senate Bill 813, which would create the California Academic Partnership Program. His testimony included the experience and promise of Project STEP's cooperative strategies.

- **November 1983--Involving More Partners**

Parent Meetings. Two meetings were held for the parents of STEP student participants at Santa Ana High School. One was held during the day and the other at night to accommodate work schedules. An introduction and description of the program was presented as well as a discussion regarding the parent's role in assisting with project goals. Approximately 200 parents attended the meetings. Regular follow-up meetings were scheduled.

Intermediate School Counselors Meeting. SAUSD intermediate school counselors met with EOP/SAA staff about the role of the intermediate school in college preparatory issues. The outcome was a recognition of the need for greater articulation and curricular alignment with the high schools. A meeting with high school counselors was planned for Spring 1984 to discuss articulation concerns.

College Board Conference in New York. Vergil Hettick from SAUSD and Antonio De Castro from UCI presented a report on STEP at a College Board conference in New York as part of the Educational EQuality Project Models Program for School/College Collaboration. Thirteen project models from across the nation were represented in an exchange of information and ideas on school-college collaboration.

- **December 1983--UCI Vice Chancellor William Lillyman Address to the Student Preparation Committee, Office of the President--Universitywide.** Among other UCI campus initiatives in curricular outreach, Lillyman cited STEP as a joint project between the UCI campus and the Santa Ana Unified School District, which he perceived "to hold special promise because it has a focus on a single school district."

- **February 1984--External Validation and Press Coverage**

President Gardner Visits UCI. UC President David Gardner addressed a group of educators during a breakfast meeting at UCI. He discussed many issues of concern in the area of improving academic preparation which related to Project STEP efforts, met with SAUSD Superintendent John Dunworth, and expressed an interest in receiving additional documentation regarding Project STEP.

College Board Visits SAUSD. Aaron Fink, Senior Advisor to the College Board's Project EQuality, visited the SAUSD to observe STEP activities in progress and to meet with school site administrators, counselors, and teachers. He commented that the STEP project was one of the most developed collaboratives in the Educational EQuality Project Models Program for School-College Collaboration.

Press Coverage. ***The Los Angeles Times*** published two articles and an editorial highlighting Project STEP. The College Board Newsletter, "Academic Connections" published an article regarding STEP. UC coverage included articles in UC Items, UC Clip Sheet, and UCI Journal. Robin Casselman, Assistant Director of EOP/SAA--Outreach, was interviewed regarding STEP on a local television program.

- **February 1984--STEP Initiatives in Progress**

Foreign Language Workshop. With support provided by Meredith Lee, UCI Dean of Undergraduate Studies, foreign language faculty Elizabeth Leeman and Ronnie LeBauer provided a workshop to SAUSD foreign language teachers describing the teaching techniques utilized at the University. A plan to have exchange visits to the secondary school and University classrooms was devised with release time for SAUSD teachers provided by the district.

Faculty Exchange and Student Visitation. Foreign language teachers from SAUSD were provided release time to visit foreign language classes at UCI. SAUSD teachers were able to observe the teaching methods employed at the University. A meeting to share their observations was planned. As part of this program, Advanced Placement foreign language students visited UCI and attended University level foreign language classes for purposes of observation. Students were pleased and their motivation was strengthened to continue their foreign language studies.

"Critical Thinking in the Humanities" Meeting. A project to work with secondary school humanities instructors to incorporate critical thinking into their curriculum was discussed by the project directors Tom Wilson and Richard Regosin, other UCI Humanities faculty, EOP/SAA staff and SAUSD representatives. The project was funded by the National Endowment for the Humanities. An agreement to select a team of SAUSD teachers for involvement in the project was reached.

Parent Meeting. The parent group held an election and selected a President, Vice President, Secretary, and Treasurer. Four committees were developed: Parent/Student Activities, Parent Advocacy, Scholarship, and Fund Raising. EOP/SAA Partnership staff were designated to serve in an advisory and support capacity. A recommendation to hire a full-time parents coordinator to focus on family involvement was made to the Director of EOP/SAA. In July, UCI became the only campus in the system to fund and appoint such a position.

• **March 1984--Preliminary Summary Report on STEP.** A report documenting the development of STEP and initial activities was submitted to the UC Office of the President by the UCI EOP/SAA Office and distributed among the project partners and interested colleagues.

• **May 1984--National Recognition for STEP**

STEP cited in *A Nation Responds,* the sequel to *A Nation at Risk*. The National Commission on Excellence in Education cited STEP in this publication as an exemplary response to improving student academic preparation. (p. 173)

"Exceptional Achievement Award" for STEP from Washington, D.C. The Council for the Advancement and Support of Education (CASE) provided additional recognition at the national level for the STEP school-college partnership model.

• **May 1984--The STEP Umbrella**

STEP Administrative Leadership Forum.

Subtitled "Focus on the Future," this Forum established the STEP "umbrella" as a tool to focus efforts on a mutual agenda. A review of activities in the academic year 1983-1984 was provided by participants in STEP including faculty, counselors and administrative staff. Notably, this forum involved a member of the SAUSD Board of Education, the SAUSD Superintendent and The Vice Chancellor of UCI, representatives from the local community college, Santa Ana College (now known as Rancho Santiago College) and from California State University, Fullerton, and a parent representative. A vigorous open discussion session produced a STEP "Wish List" of activities to sponsor in the coming year. Guest speakers included Paul Gussman from the Special Projects Division of the State Department of Education, and representatives from The College Board Project EQuality and the National Commission on Excellence in Education.

Recruitment of Teachers for UCI Summer Institutes. Professor Michael Fried had been successful in securing a grant for UCI to become a site for the California Mathematics Project, and collaborated as well as co-Principal Investigator on a proposal to NSF with Mare Taagepera, Lecturer in Chemistry, and Rita Peterson, Director, Office of Teacher Education, for the "UCI Science and Math Mentor Teacher Project." Teachers from the SAUSD and other local districts were invited to participate in six-week summer institutes and continue through the academic year to form a network of mentor teacher resources.

• **July 1984--Establishment of the First Project STEP Administrative Council.** Representatives from the SAUSD, UCI, RSC, and CSUF met to discuss plans for the future and how to proceed as the STEP Administrative Council. Dennis Galligani and Ralph Jack facilitated discussion, based in part on the summary of the May Forum "Wish Lists" in eight categories. A subcommittee was appointed to draft a statement of purpose and administrative structure, to be chaired by Carl Hartman, UCI Associate Vice Chancellor, Academic Affairs.

• **July 1984--Announcement of California Academic Partnership Program Funding in the 1984-1985 State Budget.** Chancellor Ann Reynolds from CSU Office of the Chancellor announced that the California Academic Partnership Program had been funded in the 1984-85 State budget:

> The purpose of this program is to develop cooperative efforts to improve the academic quality of secondary schools with the objective of improving the preparation of all students for college.

• **September 1984--University of California Office of the President Award.** Ralph Jack, SAUSD Assistant Superintendent, accepted this award on behalf of STEP during an annual UC systemwide Student Affirmative Action conference on September 6, 1984.

• **October 1984--STEP Administrative Council Meeting.** Dennis Galligani, UCI Assistant Vice Chancellor of Academic Affairs, acted as Chair. The purpose of this meeting was to discuss the CAPP Request for Proposals (RFP) guidelines and discuss possible plans. A Proposal Planning Committee was appointed to develop a response to the CAPP Request for Proposals due December 1.

CAPP Proposal Planning Committee Convened. A committee chaired by Marion Abbott, UCI EOP/SAA Curriculum Development Officer, was convened to develop a response to the RFP. Members included Vergil Hettick, SAUSD Director of Secondary Curriculum; Gerald Arriola, Principal, Santa Ana High School; Jackie Oakes, Program Specialist, Santa Ana High School; Cheryl Dunn, Director of the Learning Center, Rancho Santiago College; Ashley Bishop, Director of Field Services Center, CSU Fullerton; Carol Olson, Director of the UCI Writing Project and Coordinator of Project Radius; Melvin Aaron, Special Assistant, UCI Office of Academic Affairs; and Robin Casselman, Assistant Director of the UCI EOP/SAA--Outreach Office. Weekly meetings were held in November to prepare final draft for November 27 STEP Council review.

• **November 1984--STEP Council Review of Proposal to CAPP for "Project STEP: A Model of Intersegmental Collaboration."** A comprehensive plan was proposed and approved, with two essential areas of activities:
1) curricular enhancement and faculty inservice; and 2) student academic support and guidance. As stated in the proposal, "Intersegmental collaboration provides the context within which these areas are addressed and the matrix of support for students along the educational continuum. The three high schools of the SAUSD are already involved in STEP; the seven SAUSD intermediate schools will also be included. Santa Ana College, CSU Fullerton, and UC Irvine are the postsecondary institutions in the partnership."

• **December 1984--CAPP Approval for Project STEP Proposal.** The CAPP award for the project period January 1, 1985 to June 30, 1987 represented the first major external funding secured for STEP, and established the STEP Project Components structure.

• **January 1985--STEP Administrative Council Meeting.** Carl Hartman presented the draft statement of purpose and administrative structure prepared by the subcommittee for review by the Council. It was accepted with the amendment that the council shall appoint additional ex-officio members as appropriate. The proactive leadership function of the council was stressed, and the need for the provision of regular reports back to the council on project activities was acknowledged. (See page ? for the full text of the purpose statement.)

The Council members elected the following officers: Chair, Dennis Galligani (UCI); Vice Chair, Ralph Jack (SAUSD); Vice Chair (Communications): Neal Rogers (RSC).

The Council members and support staff who served on the proposal committee agreed to now serve as the CAPP Implementation Committee. Vergil Hettick, SAUSD Director of Secondary Curriculum, was appointed Chair of the CAPP Implementation Committee, and Robin Casselman, UCI Assistant Director of EOP/SAA, was appointed Vice Chair.

• **June1985--STEP Administrative Council Meeting.** Manuel Gomez was elected as the new Chair. Summer plans for each component were discussed, and the need to identify a facilitator for coordination of Summer Bridge program activities, supported by the College Board, was referred to the Implementation Committee.

Summary of Component Activities from January-June 1985 and Plans for 1985-1986

For **Critical Thinking/Reading,** Ashley Bishop reported that he and his colleague Thomas Bean, also from CSUF, had presented two ten-week workshop series, with sessions held at MacArthur Intermediate School. A review of this pilot effort produced plans to strengthen the recruitment of high school teachers into the fall course from all disciplines via departmental meetings early in the Fall. A team of six instructors would be selected from this group to continue in a spring course for stipends of $500 each, to prepare practical lesson plans and present them as mentors at a STEP Forum to teachers of reading dependent courses in Spring 1986.

Rita Peterson reported for Carol Olson, Coordinator of the **Critical Thinking/Writing Component,** regarding the ten-week inservice course conducted with Santa Ana teachers on "Fostering Critical Thinking

Skills Through Writing," and their summer project plans to develop a two-semester course in Critical Thinking/Writing for 9th grade students to be piloted at each of the high schools in the fall. Two Santa Ana English teachers were cited for their valuable contributions to the success of this component, Brenda Borron and Shari Lockman of Saddleback High School.

Plans for the academic year included an advanced course for teachers on using writing as a tool for promoting cognitive growth, and a STEP Forum for spring 1986 during which these teachers would provide an inservice for their colleagues. Meetings between the component coordinators, the assistant director of STEP, district director of secondary curriculum and English demonstration teachers were also scheduled, to insure integration of STEP activities with on-going curriculum development projects within the district.

For **Mathematics and Science Curriculum Development**, Jacquie Mobley, Director of Secondary Curriculum, reported on the district plans to review the 6-12 math curriculum in light of the 1985 California Mathematics Framework and Model Curriculum Standards adopted by the State Board of Education. Larry Chrystal, UCI visiting lecturer, agreed to work with the Math curriculum review team, to be chaired by Ana Golan, district math demonstration teacher, and joined by representatives from RSC and CSUF.

In March SAUSD teachers attended the UCI conference, "Strategies for Effective Math/Science Instruction K-12," through STEP Forums support for their release time. This conference was co-sponsored by Project Radius and the UCI Science and Mathematics Mentor Teacher Project. These staff development activities would continue through teacher participation in the UCI Summer Science Institute, the UCI Math Institute, and the combined efforts of the NSF Science and Mathematics Mentor Teacher Project. Jacquie Mobley also identified the need for science instruction inservice at the intermediate level, as a consequence of the review of the science curriculum in 1984-85 and addition of a semester of science at the 6th grade level.

Irene Malmgren reported on the STEP **Tutorial Services** pilot coordinated by RSC in Spring 1985, and the need for presentations at teachers meetings in the fall to inform more teachers about the availability of these services for students. Tutor training was being planned early to link tutoring to the Summer Bridge programs via an introduction to study groups.

For **Instructional Guidance,** Jacquie Mobley described summer project plans to develop instructional materials to support the district Comprehensive Guidance Services Curriculum, in a team effort of SAUSD teachers, counselors, and postsecondary representatives from UCI, RSC, and CSUF, which was approved by the SAUSD Board of Education. District curriculum writers included Katherine Benson, Debra Hill, Dianne Kawauchi, Jacqueline Oakes, and Wayne Snell.

Robin Casselman reported on plans for the **Summer Bridge/Parents** component orientation program scheduled for August at each of the high schools, supported by funds from the College Board. The process used in the **Student Progress Monitoring** component, coordinated by Vergil Hettick, Director of Testing and Evaluation, to assist student advisement was described.

The roster of the first STEP Administrative Council and Component Coordinators is presented in the next pages.

The STEP Administrative Council 1984-1985

Gerald Arriola, *Principal, Santa Ana High School*
Santa Ana Unified School District
Ashley Bishop, *Director, Field Services Center*
California State University, Fullerton
Coordinator, Critical Thinking/Reading
Dennis Galligani, *Assistant Vice Chancellor,*
Academic Affairs, University of California, Irvine
Chair, STEP Administrative Council
Manuel Gomez, *Director, EOP/SAA--Outreach*
University of California, Irvine
Director, CAPP Project
Carl Hartman, *Associate Vice Chancellor,*
Academic Affairs, University of California, Irvine
Chair, Committee on Council Purpose Statement
Ralph Havickhorst, *Science Teacher, Saddleback High School,*
Santa Ana Unified School District

Vergil Hettick, *Director-Testing and Evaluation*
Santa Ana Unified School District
Chair, Implementation Committee
Ralph Jack, *Assistant Superintendent for Staff Development,*
Santa Ana Unified School District
Vice Chair, STEP Administrative Council
Edward Krass, *Assistant Superintendent-Secondary Division,*
Santa Ana Unified School District
Ivan McKinney, *Principal, Valley High School*
Santa Ana Unified School District
Jacquie Mobley, *Director, Secondary Curriculum*
Santa Ana Unified School District
Nancy O'Connor, *Principal, Saddleback High School*
Santa Ana Unified School District
Rita Peterson, *Director, Office of Teacher Education*
University of California, Irvine
Neal Rogers, *Vice Chancellor, Student, Employee*
and Community Services, Rancho Santiago College
Vice Chair, STEP Admin. Council

COMPONENT COORDINATORS

Robin Casselman, *Assistant Director, EOP/SAA Outreach,*
University of California, Irvine
Co-Coordinator, Instructional Guidance
Project STEP Assistant Director and Vice Chair,
Implementation Committee
Larry Chrystal, *Visiting Lecturer, Department of Mathematics,*
University of California, Irvine
Co-Coordinator, Math/Science
Cheryl Dunn, *Director, Learning Center*
Rancho Santiago College
Coordinator, Tutorial Services
George Miller, *Lecturer, Department of Chemistry*
University of California, Irvine
Co-Coordinator, Math/Science
Jackie Oakes, *Career Guidance Specialist, Santa Ana High School,*
Santa Ana Unified School District

Co-Coordinator, Instructional Guidance

Carol Booth Olson, *Coordinator, Project Radius and UCI California Writing Project*
Coordinator, Critical Thinking/Writing

Elizabeth Rodriguez, *Program Officer, EOP/SAA, University of California, Irvine*
Coordinator, Parents in Partnership

STEP COUNCIL STAFF SUPPORT

Marion Abbott, *Curriculum Development Officer EOP/SAA Outreach, University of California, Irvine*
Chair, CAPP Proposal Committee

Joyce Friedman, *Secretary, EOP/SAA Outreach University of California, Irvine*

Jovita Quintero, *Secretary, EOP/SAA Outreach University of California, Irvine*

Project STEP: A Model of Intersegmental Collaboration: July 1985 - June 1987

This stage of the development of Project STEP can best be described in terms of a dramatic learning curve, as initial notions of university "public service" gave way to a more genuine collaboration with district educators, and as the STEP Council developed mechanisms for better coordination of activities and broader participation through creation of such groups as the STEP Faculty Forums and the Teachers Advisory Committees. In addition, formal membership in the STEP project expanded to include all seven of the SAUSD intermediate schools and Chapman College.

A chronicle of the key STEP Council and committee meetings is continued through Spring 1986 to demonstrate the evolution of these developments. The Faculty Forums in 1986-1987 are highlighted.

In the last year of this period, the strength of the STEP model, momentum of on-going activities and enthusiasm for continued growth lead project administrators to seek funding support from the Carnegie Corporation of New York. A proposal to continue implementation of various critical large-scale initiatives such as the revision of the entire 6 - 12 mathematics curriculum, and to introduce collaborative strategies to the elementary school level was approved; a grant from CAPP, which gave STEP status as a "Showcase" project for California, made full implementation of this plan possible.

• **July 1985--STEP Administrative Council Meeting.** New members were introduced, including Dr. Rudy Castruita, Assistant Superintendent, Secondary Division. Several changes in personnel for the district were noted, with corresponding changes in the Council membership. Topics for use of STEP Forum monies were proposed, including instructional guidance, use of computer technology, and science inservice. This discussion pointed out the need for a formal mechanism for review of proposed budget allocations. Such a mechanism could facilitate the project in two additional ways: 1) taking advantage of funding opportunities in the student preparation area, and 2) promoting additional institutional support for further creative efforts.

Revisions of proposed plans for 1985-1986 based upon review of the Spring pilots included a plan for utilization of more Santa Ana teachers as leaders in curriculum and staff development. In addition, the district's timeline for curriculum development in various disciplines was modified to correspond with the California State Department of Education textbook adoption cycle, which moved Language Arts curriculum planning to a 1988 implementation period, while Mathematics curriculum planning was moved up to 1985-86.

• **Summer 1985--Summer Institutes.** In addition to the summer institutes in writing, science and mathematics, STEP sponsored an English curriculum writing group to develop the 9th grade writing course for pilot implementation in 1985-1986, and Summer Bridge programs were hosted at each high school two weeks prior to the beginning of school. Also, UCI sponsored the Peer Counseling Academic Training Symposium, designed to train high school students as peer counselors to assist in disseminating information regarding college admissions procedures during the academic year.

• **September 1985--STEP Administrative Council Meeting.** Rudy Castruita described the Honors at Entrance program he initiated in

September to recognize students for their academic achievements. The draft "STEP Project Organizational Chart" was presented and used as a departure point for further discussion. The chart demonstrated the involvement of all seven intermediate school sites, the inclusion of Mountain View High School, a continuation high school, and added Chapman College, a private four-year institution in the local area led by President Buck Smith. Also reflected was the need for appointments of school-site coordinators, the Forums coordinator, and the Science component coordinator.

It was suggested and decided that the president of Chapman College be invited to appoint a representative to attend the next Council meeting. Manuel Gomez announced that the College Board had invited a STEP representative to speak at their national conference in San Francisco in October, and would be sponsoring a national forum in Mathematics through the STEP Project in the spring.

• **October 1985--CAPP Implementation Meeting.** Membership had been expanded to include all three principals of the high schools and the Director of Secondary Curriculum. Consensus was reached that the size of the committee and the dual functions of the committee--to provide periodic progress reports to project administrators and to develop proposals for STEP activities according to assessed needs--had become too unwieldy.

Component coordinators provided updates. STEP school-site facilitators for collaborative activities had been appointed at all three high schools: Jan Palmer at Saddleback; Jackie Oakes at Santa Ana; and Charlotte Jaeger at Santa Ana Valley. Jerilyn King, newly appointed as Assistant Director of Curriculum, would be responsible for counseling in the secondary division, and it was noted that the Instructional Guidance Forum, proposed as a counselors inservice regarding implementation of the guidance curriculum, would be rescheduled to accommodate Jerilyn's introduction to the project. Lucy Carr-Rollitt, the new tutor trainer, briefed the committee on the status of the tutorial services component.

For consideration under the STEP Forums component, Mike Fried, UCI Professor of Mathematics, presented information on the "Math Interview Project," designed to get at the reasons for minority student non-continuance in the math/science courses. This project had been proposed to The College Board Education EQuality Project and approved for funding.

• **November 1985--Changes in the STEP Administrative Structure.** The STEP Faculty Forums Committee, chaired by Jacquie Mobley, was established to manage the identification of partnership needs, review proposed activities and recommend budget and resource allocations. Members included the three high school principals, partner institution and component coordinator representatives, and administrators.

STEP Faculty Forums Committee. Several proposals for funding and sponsorship under STEP were reviewed, including the following: Mathematics curriculum development; Science inservice program; Thinking/Writing Follow-Up Inservice; Math Interview Project; Reading and Neurolinguistic Clinic; College Board Local Dialogue: Mathematics Leadership Forum; NSF Natural Sciences Teacher Training. The principals noted as instructional leaders they were facing enormous pressures from seemingly fragmented areas of the curriculum, but the theme of enhancing critical thinking skills runs across the disciplines. Committee recommendations focused on the potential of proposals to integrate staff development and curricular enhancement and to impact large numbers of students in the district.

• **February 1986--STEP Administrative Council Meeting.** New members were introduced: Hal Bateman, Registrar of Rancho Santiago College, and Kenneth Tye, Director of Education, Chapman College. Manuel Gomez reported on the positive outcomes of individual meetings between STEP representatives and CSU Fullerton President Cobb and RSC Chancellor Jensen. Component reports were presented and discussed.

Summary of 1986-1987 STEP Project Program Highlights

• **March and August 1986--Parents Conferences with Paulo Freire.** A series of community dialogues hosted at Rancho Santiago College with the renown Brazilian educator Paulo Freire was initiated in 1986.

Parents and families of students in the Santa Ana district attended these sessions in large numbers.

• **April 1986--Mathematics Leadership Dialogue.** This faculty forum assisted in the development of a core of SAUSD mathematics instructional leaders from each of the high schools and intermediate schools who were conversant with the Model Curriculum Standards in Mathematics, and could then introduce these new concepts to all of the secondary level mathematics teachers. The "Mathematics Leadership Dialogue," co-sponsored by The College Board's Education EQuality Project, convened a total of eighty participants including twenty-one SAUSD mathematics teachers and forty-four faculty and administrators from STEP institutions. Representatives from ten districts and agencies such as the Orange County and State Department's of Education were also invited to observe. Jaime Escalante was the keynote speaker.

• **May 1986--STEP Presentation to the Rancho Santiago College Board of Trustees.** STEP representatives including Lucy Carr-Rollitt, the coordinator of tutor training for the STEP Tutorial Services Component and the Project Director Manuel Gomez, provided an overview of STEP to the RSC Board of Trustees.

• **May - December 1986--Expansion of Project STEP.** In May UCI's EOP/SAA Office submitted a proposal for expansion of its Early Outreach Partnership Program based on the model of academic collaboration established in STEP, and received a permanent grant to expand student services into the Los Angeles area schools.

In August, Gloria De Necochea, from the Carnegie Corporation of New York, visited with Project STEP representatives to discuss possible funding under the "Education: Science, Technology, and the Economy" program.

• **November 1986--The Achievement Council Principals Conference.** This conference, hosted at UCI, marked the beginning of a working relationship between Project STEP and The Achievement Council on such initiatives as Project TEAMS: "Teaching Excellence for Achievement in Minority Schools."

• **December 1986-February 1987--Proposal Submitted to the Carnegie Corporation of New York.** In December, a request was submitted to the Carnegie Corporation for "The Next STEP." This proposed to refine the model in Santa Ana and test it by developing adaptations with two additional minority dominant school districts (Compton and Long Beach Unified School Districts) and their complementary postsecondary institutions (Compton Community College; CSU Dominguez Hills; Long Beach City College, CSU Long Beach). A funding decision by the Carnegie Corporation in February granted an award to strengthen the Santa Ana STEP model and expand it into the elementary school level, which resulted in the 1987-1990 fourth phase of "Project STEP: A Partnership for the Advancement of Learning."

• **February 1987--STEP Counselors Conference hosted at CSU Fullerton.** A STEP Counselors Conference was held in February under the leadership of the new district coordinator for counseling, Ramon Reza, Assistant Director of Secondary Curriculum, who joined the district staff in December 1986, and Valerie Bordeaux, Assistant Director, CSUF University Outreach and Relations with Schools. Ramon continued the work of Jerilyn King, his predecessor, for inservice training of the district counselors regarding the "Comprehensive Guidance Curriculum," in collaboration with college outreach staff.

A series of planning meetings scheduled at each of the STEP institutions in the fall culminated in this partnership-wide conference. Counselors from all levels--intermediate school, high school, community college and four-year college--met together for the first time to discuss guidance strategies to increase student transition to postsecondary education.

• **April 1987--Showcase Proposal Submitted to CAPP by Project STEP.** This request built upon support from the Carnegie award to complete a ten-component program outlined for the STEP partners focusing on student preparation in mathematics and science. Another significant aspect of the grant as a "Showcase" project for CAPP were responsibilities to disseminate the partnership model developed, and to extend the model to the Compton Unified School District and local colleges in the third year of funding.

July 1987--Final Three-Year Report Submitted to CAPP.
This report discussed the activities and outcomes of Project STEP in terms of five principles that project administrators believed to be responsible for this successful academic collaboration: 1) long-term commitment; 2) an administrative council structure that formalized the relationships; 3) a focused action plan aligned with long-term institutional goals; 4) sufficient comprehensive scope to address the three objectives of curriculum enhancement, professional development, and student academic guidance; and 5) adequate resources, human and fiscal.

The STEP Administrative Council 1985-1987

Gerald Arriola, *Principal, Santa Ana High School*
Santa Ana Unified School District
Hal Bateman, *Registrar, Rancho Santiago College*
--new member February 1986
Ashley Bishop, *Director, Field Services Center*
California State University, Fullerton
Coordinator, Critical Thinking/Reading
Robin Casselman, *Assistant Director, EOP/SAA Outreach,*
University of California, Irvine
Assistant Director, Project STEP
Rudy Castruita, *Assistant Superintendent,*
Santa Ana Unified School District
--new member July 1985
Cheryl Dunn, *Director, Learning Center*
Rancho Santiago College
Coordinator, Tutorial Services
Dennis Galligani, *Assistant Vice Chancellor,*
Academic Affairs, University of California, Irvine
Manuel Gomez, *Director, EOP/SAA--Outreach*
University of California, Irvine
Director, Project STEP
Carl Hartman, *Associate Vice Chancellor,*
Academic Affairs, University of California, Irvine

Ralph Havickhorst, *Science Teacher, Saddleback High School, Santa Ana Unified School District*
Vergil Hettick, *Director-Testing and Evaluation Santa Ana Unified School District*
Chair, Implementation Committee
Ralph Jack, *Assistant Superintendent for Staff Development, Santa Ana Unified School District*
Vice Chair, STEP Administrative Council
Edward Krass, *Superintendent, Santa Ana Unified School District*
Murdo MacLeod, *Principal, Valley High School Santa Ana Unified School District*
--new member July 1985
Jacquie Mobley, *Director, Secondary Curriculum Santa Ana Unified School District*
Chair, Faculty Forums Committee
Nancy O'Connor, *Principal, Saddleback High School Santa Ana Unified School District*
Rita Peterson, *Director, Office of Teacher Education University of California, Irvine*
Kenneth Tye, *Director of Education, Chapman College*
--new member February 1986

COMPONENT COORDINATORS

Valerie Bordeaux, *Assistant Director, University Outreach and Admissions, California State University, Fullerton*
Chair, STEP Counselors Conference Planning Committee
Lucy Carr-Rollitt, *Learning Specialist, Learning Center, Rancho Santiago College*
Larry Chrystal, *Visiting Lecturer, Department of Mathematics, University of California, Irvine*
Co-Coordinator, Math/Science
David Guzman, *Dean of Students, Rancho Santiago College*
George Miller, *Lecturer, Department of Chemistry University of California, Irvine*

Co-Coordinator, Math/Science
Carol Booth Olson, *Coordinator, Project Radius and UCI California Writing Project,*
Coordinator, Critical Thinking/Writing
Ramon Reza, *Assistant Director, Secondary Curriculum, Santa Ana Unified School District*
Coordinator, Instructional Guidance

SAUSD HIGH SCHOOL STEP FACILITATORS

SADDLEBACK:	Diane Kawauchi, *Science Teacher (1987)*
	Jan Palmer, *English Teacher (Valley High, 1987)*
SANTA ANA:	John Acuna, *Counselor*
	Jackie Oakes, *Career Guidance Specialist*
VALLEY:	Charlotte Jaeger, *English Teacher*

SAUSD INTERMEDIATE SCHOOL PRINCIPALS AND STEP FACILITATORS

CARR: Vincent Tafolla,	Fredell Scott, Diane Becker
LATHROP: Richard Rankin	Robert Segura, Richard Kempf
MACARTHUR: Thomas Reasin	Lorna Shelby
MCFADDEN: Judy Duesterberg	Barbara Mitchell, Kathy Benson
SIERRA: Dan Salcedo	Ann Okine, Maria Colmenares
SPURGEON: Ernest Raugewitz	Velina Esparza, Beverly Hill
WILLARD: Greg Rankin	Dolores Witt, Joy Fromong

EOP/SAA--OUTREACH STAFF SUPPORT TO PROJECT STEP

Adisa Anderson, *Junior High Partnership*
Marco Banda, *Academic Enrichment Program*
Helen Daniel, *Senior High Partnership*
Cheryl Dearman, *High School Recruitment*
Marsheila de Van, *Junior High Partnership*
Joyce Friedman, *Secretary*
Cathy Goodman, *Data Coordination,*
Imelda Hermosillo, *Senior High Partnership*
Darlene Mims, *Data Support*
Gerardo Mouet, *Assistant Director, EOP*
Elizabeth Rodriguez, *Parents in Partnership*
Nham Tripodes, *Secretary*
Betty Watanabe-Isa, *Seniors Follow-Up*
Randall Wold, *Research Analyst*

Project STEP: "A Partnership for the Advancement of Learning:" 1987--1990.

The ten-component structure and activities of this phase of STEP, supported by the CAPP Showcase and Carnegie Corporation of New York grants, are described in various chapters. Activities were designed to support each of the five overall goals of Project STEP: enhancement of mathematics/science instruction, development of future teachers, further development of the formal model of collaboration, project dissemination efforts, and institutionalization of the partnership. A few of the major contributions of these components will be highlighted here.

To assist the Project Directors and Council in oversight coordination of these components, two Associate Directors were appointed: Jacquie Mobley from the SAUSD, and Robin Casselman from UCI.

GOAL ONE: IMPROVED ACADEMIC PREPARATION FOR ALL STUDENTS, AND PARTICULARLY IMPROVED UNDERREPRESENTED MINORITY STUDENT PREPARATION IN MATHEMATICS AND SCIENCE.

Component One: (Integrating) Mathematics/Science Instructional Teams. Under the direction of Larry Chrystal, UCI Math Lecturer and Assistant to the Dean, Department of Mathematics, three teams of math and science teachers collaborated with post-secondary faculty in 1987-1988 to develop lesson plans which integrate the teaching of math and science concepts. On April 14, a STEP faculty forum on "Integrating Mathematics and Science Instruction" was held at UCI, during which these teachers demonstrated these new instructional strategies to a group of their peers from each of the 11 SAUSD secondary schools. For the first time in a STEP faculty forum, SAUSD students from the intermediate and high school level were brought in to create demonstration classrooms. On the same day, these students were also provided with a campus tour and introduction to the UCI nuclear reactor laboratory. Due to the success of this effort, new teams of math/science teachers at many of the schools have been formally and informally created, which signals an unprecedented level of cooperation among the teachers of math and science in the district.

Component Two: Intersegmental Mathematics and Science Curriculum Task Force Committees/Faculty Forums. Under the direction of Dr. Jacquie Mobley, SAUSD Director of Curriculum, this committee continued its work on curricular review and revision in mathematics and science, and on the development of staff development workshops and resource guides. One milestone in particular stands out, the elimination of "BIM" classes in 1988-89, "Basic Instruction in Mathematics," which will enhance the likelihood of students ultimately enrolling in college preparatory mathematics.

New members have joined this intersegmental committee, which now includes Ana Golan and Charlotte Griswold from the SAUSD, Luis Ortiz Franco from Chapman College, David Pagni from CSUF, and Larry Chrystal from UCI. Members of this group shared their experience as secondary/ postsecondary collaborators in a panel presentation by STEP at the May 27-28 Symposium on "Equity Issues in Mathematics and Science Achievement" sponsored by the Southwest Center for Educational Equity.

Component Three: Family Math for Kindergarten through Sixth Grade. Under the direction of David Pagni, CSUF Professor of Mathematics, and Ana Garza, Home/School Coordinator of Project SAFEMAP and Associate Professor of Education, CSUF, this component of Project STEP met with a high level of success at the elementary level (training teachers from 20 of the elementary schools), and introduced the program to teachers from five of the intermediate schools in the district. The "Family Math" program, developed by the EQUALS Project and the Lawrence Hall of Science at UC Berkeley under the auspices of a FIPSE grant, trains teachers to work with parents and their children to increase family interest and participation in mathematics learning.

GOAL TWO: DEVELOPMENT OF FUTURE TEACHERS IN MATHEMATICS AND SCIENCE, ESPECIALLY TEACHERS FROM ETHNIC BACKGROUNDS UNDERREPRESENTED IN HIGHER EDUCATION.

Component Seven: Cooperative Learning Labs and Leaders in Mathematics and Science. In 1987-88, the highlight of this component, which has been a major contributor to Project STEP successes since its inception in the spring of 1985, was the expansion to one site at the intermediate school level and the extension of tutorial services to include science courses at the high school level. Under the direction of Dr. Cheryl Dunn, Director of the Learning Center at Rancho Santiago College, and with extraordinary administrative support from Lucy Carr-Rollitt, efforts in the past year included the recruitment of several ethnic minority college students interested in teaching, to provide them an opportunity to gain experience in the field. The work of this component is regarded at a very high level by the school-site leadership; with the support of the principals, STEP funding for these services was continued into 1989-1990.

GOAL THREE: (FURTHER) DEVELOPMENT OF THE COMPREHENSIVE MODEL OF INTERSEGMENTAL COLLABORATION

Component Nine: Project STEP Faculty Forums. In the spring of 1988, during the period of SAUSD faculty salary negotiations and potential strike action, the STEP Teacher Advisory Committee was formed to insure appropriate input from faculty concerning future Project STEP efforts involving teachers. In hindsight, this new committee appears to be a major contribution of the 1988-89 academic year, in the strength it lends to the STEP model. Although there has always been one teacher representative on the STEP Council, this subcommittee affords SAUSD teachers a formal vehicle through which to approach the Council, which is essential for broadening the range of involvement, communication and influence of teachers directly in shaping the STEP partnership.

Hank Montelongo, appointed to the committee as a representative of the Santa Ana Educators Association and now a member of the STEP Council representing teachers along with Ana Golan, expressed his optimism that the STEP Teacher Advisory Committee will enhance the dissemination of information regarding STEP initiatives to the teachers in the district and provide an opportunity for more teacher input. With the assistance of this group, for example, STEP Faculty Forum support for the district's review and revision of the ESL program was carried out this year.

GOAL FOUR: DISSEMINATION OF MODEL TO THE INTER-SEGMENTAL ACADEMIC COMMUNITY

Project STEP Brochure. Under the leadership of Gerardo Mouet, who served as the STEP Coordinator in fall 1987, a brochure highlighting the support of the STEP partner institution CEO's and the work of the STEP Administrative Council was produced.

CAPP Showcase Conferences. In the spring of 1988 STEP hosted two "CAPP Showcase" conferences in Berkeley and Fresno. Evaluations indicated outstanding reception to these "Dialogues," which focused on critical issues in collaboration and provided an excellent forum for the review of CAPP objectives. Participants represented all sectors of the educational continuum.

Establishment of the Compton Council for Academic Achievement. On August 4, 1987 the initial meeting of the "Compton Council for Academic Achievement was convened by Compton Unified School District Superintendent, Ted Kimbrough, with representatives from Compton College, CSU Dominguez Hills, CSU Pomona, and UCI. The pace of this development and the leadership the district has taken suggests the viability of the model.

GOAL FIVE: INSTITUTIONALIZATION OF THE MODEL THROUGH ESTABLISHMENT OF A PERMANENT INTERSEGMENTAL PARTNERSHIP

STEP Data Management Committee. The development by the STEP Data Management Committee of joint partner data collection efforts and follow-up and tracking methodologies for SAUSD students to demonstrate project impacts has been a major contribution.

SAUSD Comprehensive Guidance Curriculum. Development of this curriculum and the articulation of guidance services it accomplishes were identified as initial STEP goals; it is now credited as one the STEP's major achievements. In four years the curriculum has been expanded to include grade levels 6 through 12, and a resource guide has been produced to assist implementation of the lessons by counselors within Language Arts and Social Studies classrooms.

October 1989 STEP Council Objectives and Task Forces.
At the initiative of the SAUSD Superintendent this fall, a statement of "STEP Council Objectives" written by district personnel was adopted. The statement notes that "Participation in the STEP Council is based on the following assumptions: 1) that the members of the Council are here to represent their whole institution; 2) that where possible we develop recommendations on a K - 12 basis; 3) that the enrollment of limited English proficient students has increased to 56% of the District's total

enrollment and that all recommendations emerging from the Council will take this into account; and 4) that the Board of Education has directed that all District programs actively promote parent involvement."

At the October meeting, the STEP Council was expanded to include several representatives from the elementary division, and four task forces of the Council were established, to be convened by district personnel. This marks a watershed in the evolution of the STEP partnership. The district's latest expression of ownership of STEP represents the clearest evidence to date of the accomplishment of this objective--the institutionalization of these relationships.

A compilation of the 1987-1990 STEP Administrative Council rosters is provided below.

The STEP Administrative Council 1987-1990

Sy Abrego, *Director, Student Academic Services and Outreach, California State University, Fullerton*

Remi Alvarez, *Principal, Mountain View High School*
--new member October 1989

Gerald Arriola, *Principal, Century High School Santa Ana Unified School District*

John Bennett, *Assistant Superintendent, Elementary Division, Santa Ana Unified School District*
--new member October 1989.

Joan Bissell, *Assistant Director, Office of Teacher Education University of California, Irvine*

Diana Blazey, *Principal, Madison Elementary*
--new member October 1989

Robin Casselman, *Associate Director, EOP/SAA Outreach,*
Associate Director, Project STEP

Rudy Castruita, *Superintendent, Santa Ana Unified School District*
Director, Project STEP

Zeff Dena, *Assistant Director,Secondary Curriculum Santa Ana Unified School District*

--new member October 1988.

Susan Despenas, *Deputy Administrator, Elementary Division. Santa Ana Unified School District*
--new member October 1989

Judy Duesterberg, *Principal, Valley High School Santa Ana Unified School District*
--new member October 1989

Cheryl Dunn, *Director, Learning Center Rancho Santiago College*
Coordinator, Tutorial Services

Dennis Galligani, *Assistant Vice Chancellor, Academic Affairs, University of California, Irvine*

Ana Golan, *Mathematics Demonstration Teacher, Teacher/Curriculum Specialist, Santa Ana Unified School District*
Teacher Advisory Representative to 1988-89; Co-coordinator Component Two: Math/Science Curriculum Committees.

Manuel Gomez, *Assistant Vice Chancellor, Academic Affairs--Student Affirmative Action and Director, EOP/SAA--Outreach, University of California, Irvine*
Director, Project STEP

Howard Haas, *Principal, Willard Intermediate School Santa Ana Unified School District*
Chair, STEP Task Force on Tutoring

Carmela Harvey, *Coordinator, Student Academic Outreach Services and University Outreach, California State University, Fullerton*

Andrew Hernandez, *Principal, Santa Ana High School Santa Ana Unified School District*

Edward Hernandez, *Vice Chancellor Rancho Santiago College*
--new member October 1989

Vergil Hettick, *Director, Testing and Evaluation Santa Ana Unified School District*
Chair, Data Management Committee

Cathy Makin, *Principal, Spurgeon Intermediate,*
--member 1987 to 1989.

Jacquie Mobley, *Director, Secondary Curriculum*
Santa Ana Unified School District
Associate Director, Project STEP; resigned July 88.
Hank Montelongo, *Teacher, McFadden Intermediate School*
Santa Ana Unified School District
Teacher Advisory Representative to Council 88-90.
Bob Nelson, *Principal, Saddleback High School*
Santa Ana Unified School District
Chair, STEP Task Force on Student Outreach
Nancy O'Connor, *Assistant Superintendent, Secondary Division,*
Santa Ana Unified School District
Luis Ortiz Franco, *Professor of Mathematics,*
Chapman College
David Pagni, *Professor of Mathematics,*
California State University, Fullerton
Coordinator, Component Three: Family Math
Phil Quon, *Director,Secondary Curriculum*
Santa Ana Unified School District
Chair, STEP Task Force on Science
Greg Rankin, *Principal, Lathrop Intermediate*
--new member October 1989
Ramon Reza, *Assistant to the Superintendent*
Santa Ana Unified School District
Coordinator, Component Ten: Instructional Guidance;
Chair, STEP Task Force on Drug Prevention.
Nadine Rodriguez, *Principal, Washington Elementary*
--new member October 1989
Dan Salcedo, *Principal, Sierra Intermediate*
--new member October 1989
Marge Sawyer, *Director, Elementary Curriculum,*
Santa Ana Unified School District
--new member October 1989
Kenneth Tye, *Director of Education,*
Chapman College
--new member February 1986; resigned December 1989.

COMPONENT COORDINATORS AND STAFF ASSOCIATES

Eric Arakaki, *Administrative Assistant, EOP/SAA--Outreach, University of California, Irvine*
Deborah Brandon, *Assistant Director, EOP/SAA--Outreach, University of California, Irvine*
Lucy Carr-Rollitt, *Learning Specialist, Learning Center, Rancho Santiago College*
Larry Chrystal, *Assistant to the Dean, Department of Mathematics, University of California, Irvine*
Lesley Danziger, Assistant Administrative Analyst, EOP/SAA--Outreach, *University of California, Irvine*
David Guzman, *Dean of Students, Rancho Santiago College*
George Miller, *Lecturer, Department of Chemistry*

SAUSD HIGH SCHOOL STEP FACILITATORS

SADDLEBACK:	Diane Kawauchi, *Science Teacher (1987)*
	Jan Palmer, *English Teacher (Valley High, 1987)*
SANTA ANA:	Jackie Oakes, *Career Guidance Specialist*
VALLEY:	Lynn Kramer, *Coordinator, Valley Academy*

APPENDIX B

Select Projects and Organizations Which Support Collaborative and Partnership Efforts

CALIFORNIA ACADEMIC PARTNERSHIP PROGRAM (CAPP)

The California State University
Office of the Chancellor
400 Golden Shore, Suite 132
Long Beach, CA 90802-4275
Deborah Hancock, Statewide Director
(213) 590-5379

California Academic Partnership Program (CAPP) provides an avenue by which California school districts and postsecondary institutions can work together to create improved learning, academic preparation, and access opportunities for students in middle schools and high schools, so that more students, especially those underrepresented on postsecondary campuses, can successfully complete baccalaureate degree programs.

CENTER FOR EDUCATIONAL RENEWAL

University of Washington
Miller Hall
Seattle, WA 98195
John I. Goodlad, Director
(206) 543-6162

Founded in 1985, the Center for Educational Renewal conducts research and development activities pertaining to the simultaneous reconstruction of K-12 schools and the preparation of educators. The Center is part of the College of Education, at the University of Washington,

Seattle, Washington. The Center for Educational Renewal serves as a kind of hub for fourteen student/university partnerships in as many states: Arizona, Arkansas, California, Colorado, Connecticut, Hawaii, Indiana, Maine, Michigan, New York, Utah, Virginia, Washington, and Wyoming. Each consists of at least one university and serves surrounding school districts. In several settings, the school district involved up to a third of the K-12 population in that state. The Center provides technical support, evaluation, and ongoing inquiry into the concept of symbiotic school/university partnerships and the implementation of this concept in the fourteen settings.

COALITION FOR ESSENTIAL SCHOOLS

Brown University
Education Department Box 1938
Providence, Rhode Island 02912
(401) 863-3384
Theodore Sizer

Established in 1984 as a high school-university partnership, the Coalition of Essential Schools is devoted to strengthening the learning of students by reforming each school's priorities and simplifying its structure. Brown University joined in this partnership with schools that are diverse in character, geographically dispersed and representative of both the public and private sectors. Each school evolves a plan appropriate to its own setting. Coalition schools hold in common a set of nine common principles that give focus to their effort.

THE ACHIEVEMENT COUNCIL

The Achievement Council
1016 Castro Street
Oakland, CA 94607
M. Susana Navarro, Ph.D., Executive Director
(415) 839-4647

Since its inception in 1985, The Achievement Council has worked intensely with predominantly minority schools through a variety of initiatives designed to raise student achievement. Through its many initiatives, the Council and its university partners have created opportunities for administrators and teachers from schools across California to come together to discuss problems and solutions. Participants hear from representatives of "Schools on the Move" and learn both about effective practices and the change process. They also learn about the many resources available to them as they seek to improve their schools. Among the Council's major initiatives are Project Teams, The Achievement League, and the San Francisco Collaborative.

THE EDUCATIONAL EQUALITY PROJECT

The College Board
45 Columbus Avenue
New York, New York 10023-6992
Donald Stewart, President, College Board
Adrienne Bailey, Vice President, Academic Affairs
(212) 713-8000

The Educational EQuality Project Models Program for School-College Collaboration is a national network of collaborative projects between high schools and colleges. Its members share a commitment to expanding and diversifying the pool of students who are academically well prepared to enter and succeed in higher education. The EQ Models Program includes 17 distinct partnerships in different parts of the country. The program as a whole explores the variety of ways in which collaboration between secondary and higher education can advance such equity and excellence in education.

THE NATIONAL DIRECTORY OF SCHOOL-COLLEGE PARTNERSHIPS: CURRENT MODELS AND PRACTICES

Published in 1987 by American Association of Higher Education, to be updated in 1990; sponsored by National Association of Secondary School Principals.

American Association of Higher Education
Syracuse University
Project Advance
111 Waverly Avenue, Suite 200
Syracuse, NY 13244-2320
(315) 443-2404
Frank Wilbur, Director

The directory contains abstracts of over one hundred and fifty partnership programs which represent fifteen categories of program types and a list of 1,042 programs referenced by program categories. Program categories include, for example, Tutoring Programs, Reservice/Training New Teachers, Minority, Disadvantages and At Risk Students. An electronic data base provides further information about each program in the directory.

A NATIONAL PROJECT IN SUPPORT OF ACADEMIC ALLIANCES

American Association for Higher Education (AAHE)
One Dupont Circle, Suite 600
Washington, D.C. 20036
Paula Bagasao, National Project Director
(202) 293-6440

The American Association for Higher Education (AAHE) has established a National Project in Support of Academic Alliances to serve as an organizational base support school/college collaborations. Wide participation and collaboration in the Academic Alliances movement by school and college faculty is a powerful force in strengthening the professional and in enhancing the quality of teaching and learning in the disciplines.

PENNSYLVANIA ACADEMY FOR THE PROFESSION OF TEACHING

Pennsylvania Academy for the Profession of Teaching
University Center at Harrisburg
2986 North Second Street
Harrisburg, PA 17110
Charles Clevenger, Executive Director
Susan Arisman, Associate Director
(717) 787-9565

The Pennsylvania Academy for the Profession of Teaching is an initiative of the State System of Higher Education which seeks "to improve teaching and learning at all levels of education and to enhance teaching as a profession." Through various projects, the Academy collaborates between and among faculty in the arts, sciences and in teacher education. This includes working with public and independent colleges and universities, and the basic and higher education communities.

UNIVERSITY OF CALIFORNIA EARLY ACADEMIC OUTREACH PROGRAM

University of California
Office of the President
Admissions and Outreach
317 University Hall
University of California, Berkeley
Berkeley, CA 94720
Ed Apodaca
(415) 642-5769

Since 1975, the UC Early Academic Outreach Program has coordinated programs which encourage underrepresented minority students to increase their educational aspirations and improve their academic preparation for University-level work. EAO has the responsibility to assist secondary schools, increase the number of SAA student who achieve UC eligibility, to increase students' and parents' awareness of postsecondary opportunities available and to motivate students to challenge themselves academically. EAO's services are based on the knowledge that we as educators must work collaboratively with school districts, schools and postsecondary institutions in order to ensure students benefit from the expertise and resources of the entire educational community.

WESTERN INTERSTATE COMMISSION FOR HIGHER EDUCATION (WICHE)

WICHE Publications
P.O. Drawer P
Boulder, Colorado 80301-9752
(303) 497-0290
Richard Jonsen, Executive Director

WICHE is a regional public agency established to promote resource sharing, collaboration, and cooperative planning among the western states and their colleges and universities. WICHE's mission centers on strengthening educational opportunities for students through expanded access to programs. WICHE is governed by a Commission appointed by the governors of the member and affiliated states. WICHE's mission centers on strengthening educational opportunities for students through expanded access to programs; assisting policymakers in dealing with higher education and human resource issues through research and analysis; and fostering cooperative planning and effective use of resources.

APPENDIX C

ANNOTATED BIBLIOGRAPHY

Selected Books
Relevant to the Development of Academic Partnerships

For too long the various educational sectors have labored in isolation to address educational challenges and concerns. Ironically, it is only after a series of national reports warning of the problems facing the American educational system that the benefits of forming partnerships across the educational continuum and between the business and academic sectors are being fully recognized. The current literature on partnerships provides a rich resource of ideas with which to approach the educational challenges of the present and the future. In particular, current partnerships address urgent concerns related to our rapidly changing demographics and the needs of an emerging multicultural, multilingual society and the pressing need to produce skilled scientists and computer scientists to maintain American economic competitiveness. There is a wealth of literature related to specific partnership programs and ideas about approaching these educational challenges. We have included a brief annotated bibliography as a resource for potential partnerships.

Atkin, Myron J. and Atkin, A. ***Improving Science Education Through Local Alliances.*** (1989). A Report to the Carnegie Corporation of New York. Santa Cruz, CA: Network Publications.

As indicated by the title, this report analyzes the role of partnerships and other collaborative efforts in the improvement of science education in the K-12 schools. The first part of the book describes different types of alliances with the K-12 sector, including alliances with the corporate world, with universities, with museums, and with different combined groups, described here as "third party agencies." The second part of the book analyzes a couple of basic problems which the researchers perceived with these alliances for improved science education: namely, their durability as alliances and the quality of science instruction that they promote. The book concludes with some recommendations from successful partnerships, including Project STEP.

California Commission on Educational Quality. Report to the Governor. (1988). Sacramento, CA: Governor's Office.

This report begins by stating that, despite a significant increase in spending, one-third of California's schools are failing to meet student achievement goals set for them through recent school reforms. Furthermore, population projections indicate that California elementary and secondary schools will have over 1.2 million additional students by the end of the century. A large number of these additional students will be poor, or immigrants or limited English speaking. In order to meet these educational challenges, the report outlines 69 specific recommendations organized in five general areas: setting and formalizing goals and standards; monitoring and assessing progress toward those goals; involving parents, teachers and the community with the student in the school; making educational programs more efficient; and providing assistance to schools and school districts. The report emphasizes the need for greater cooperation and support among K-12 educators, administrators, and parents; however, the possibility of intersegmental partnerships is not explored. In fact, academic partnerships between the postsecondary and K-12 sectors can add an important support role and fill the gap between local and state intervention into districts experiencing the academic challenges described here.

Comer, James P. ***School Power.*** (1980). New York, NY: The Free Press, A Division of Macmillan Publishing Co.

School Power describes the development of a collaboration begun in 1968 between the Yale Child-Study Center and the New Haven public school system. The collaboration addressed the problem of low academic achievement among inner-city minority school children. The two elementary schools which were initially selected for the program not only demonstrated the lowest academic achievement in the New Haven school system at that time, but also reported serious behavioral and attendance problems among students, low morale among teachers, and dissatisfaction on the part of parents and community workers. The program aimed to improve academic achievement and the social and psychological climate of the two elementary school partners and to provide the clinicians with the opportunity to observe children in a public school setting. The book describes the difficult beginnings of the collaboration, including the withdrawal of one of the elementary schools, and the final success of the collaboration in attaining its goals. Along the way, the collaboration developed some model program components for enhancing the self esteem and social skills of disadvantaged elementary school children. The elementary school that remained in the collaboration went on to score among the top third of all schools in the city in academic achievement.

This collaborative program provides useful advice for other partnerships in terms of both program development and organization. Comer emphasizes the importance of assisting disadvantaged students in the earliest grades in order to compensate for experiences they cannot bring to the educational process. He also stresses the importance of involving parents in schooling and of providing school teachers with training in mental health and child development. He advises future collaborations of the importance of maintaining an atmosphere of equality and collegiality in the relations between college and school representatives and of the need to understand and respect each other's differences in terms of methodologies and assumptions. The title of the book, ***Schoolpower,*** reinforces a constant theme in the book of eliminating power struggles between school participants and reasserting the power of the school as a cohesive and positive force in the lives of children.

Education and Urban Society, November 1986, Volume 19, Number 1, Sage Publications.

This issue of ***Education and Urban Society*** is devoted to an examination of school-university collaborations. Adrienne Bailey, in her article "More Than Good Intentions: Building a Network of Collaboratives," describes the development of the "Educational EQuality Project Models Program for School-College Collaboration," formed by the College Board. This network of high school-college collaborative projects is a central component of the College Board's Educational EQuality Project (EQ), which is committed to strengthening the quality of secondary education and ensuring equal access to postsecondary education for all students. Bailey describes pertinent issues in a variety of collaborative models and concludes with lessons learned about both local collaboration and the creation of a network of collaboratives.

Juan Lara and Ruth Mitchell in "The Seamless Web: The Interdependence of Educational Institutions," describe the efforts of the Center for Academic Interinstitutional Programs (CAIP) at the University of California, Los Angeles, to deal with issues of student preparation for college in innovative and meaningful ways. They provide a historical perspective to the design of their various programs leading to the Transfer Alliance Program (TAP) in conjunction with the community colleges. The article discusses issues and lessons learned from these programs and the authors' future goal of reshaping teacher education, both for preservice and professional development.

Mary Morison Nur, in "The Role of Research-Oriented Universities in School Change," details the school-university partnership based at Stanford University. She describes several features that characterize the Study of Stanford and the Schools, and discusses how the collaborative process contributes to the link between research and practice.

James Vivian, in "Issues in Establishing and Developing an Educational Collaboration: The Yale-New Haven Experience," provides background surrounding several aspects of the nationally acclaimed educational collaborative program between Yale and the town of New Haven. Vivian shares with readers the processes involved in determining aims, activities, and schedules, and in the invention of terminology to match program goals.

Finally, Bernard Gifford, in "The Evolution of the School-University Partnership for Educational Renewal (SUPER)," describes the development of the SUPER Project. This collaboration, between sixteen school sites and the School of Education at the University of California Berkeley, encompasses a wide range of educational components with the general purpose of developing "practice-sensitive researchers and research-sensitive practitioners."

Galligani, D.J. (1987). ***Effective Relationships for School/College Partnerships: A Qualitative Evaluation of the Curriculum Enhancement Projects Participating in the California Academic Partnership Program 1984-1987.*** California State University, Long Beach, CA: California Academic Partnership Program.

This report is a qualitative evaluation of the first twenty joint school/college curriculum enhancement partnership projects which were funded by CAPP to improve academic preparation. The report describes the experiences, insights and recommendations of the partners involved in these projects in the following areas: characteristics which contribute to effective partnerships, especially in terms of administrative structures and faculty-to-faculty interaction; successful ways to achieve curriculum enhancement; approaches to reaching specific project goals, such as targeting underrepresented students, institutionalizing project activities, disseminating project information, and developing evaluation measurements. The report, written in an outline format, is extremely focused and tightly packed with specific recommendations culled from the experience of the twenty partnership projects.

Gross, T.L. ***Partners in Education: How Colleges Can Work with Schools to Improve Teaching and Learning.*** (1988). San Francisco, CA: Jossey-Bass.

Based on his experience with the SUNY (State University of New York) Purchase, Westchester School Partnership, Professor Gross offers suggestions to potential partnership leaders, particularly those from the postsecondary sector. He provides a brief overview of several successful partnerships, explains how partnerships can be organized and administered, discusses funding possibilities, and concludes with some interesting resource lists, such as a list of arguments to present to prospective school districts, universities, and corporation. The SUNY, Purchase Westchester partnership developed some interesting collaborative experiences with business. For example, IBM executives provide leadership seminars for the school district administrators and local corporations agreed to hire district guidance counselors for a month's summer employment to gain job experiences. This type of partnership differs from project STEP in its orientation towards postsecondary administration and in its concentration on training teachers and administrators through external programs and university-based institutes. Nevertheless, there is much valuable shared experience here.

National Science Board Commission on Precollege Education in Mathematics, Science and Technology. (1983). ***Educating Americans for the 21st Century.*** Washington, D.C.: National Science Foundation.

This report spells out a detailed plan of action for all sectors of society to address the "very serious problems" facing America's elementary and secondary educational systems in mathematics, science and technology. The report recommends several strategies to improve education in these areas. Partnerships with business, government and academia are encouraged to assist in teacher preparation and curriculum development. Although not dealing directly with partnerships, the urgency of this report and the breadth of improvements that it recommends clearly indicate the need for increased partnership enterprises to support the K-12 sector.

Editors: Odell, M. and Mock, J. (1989). ***A Crucial Agenda: Making Colleges Work Better for Minority Students.*** Boulder, CO: Western Interstate Commission for Higher Education.

This report contains a series of papers by educational leaders and scholars on the topic of how best to serve the academic needs of underrepresented minorities. The report begins very effectively by reminding the reader that these so-called minorities will comprise one-third of the entire U.S. population by the turn of the century. Using the experience of the Southwestern states as a model, the different papers explore this "crucial national agenda" from a variety of perspectives. Throughout the papers, certain themes are emphasized: the need to develop an attitude of success among both minority students and the policy makers, institutional leaders and faculty who serve them; the need for the colleges and universities to shift their emphasis from pure research to the integration of multicultural perspectives into disciplines and teaching methods; the need to develop partnerships between the K-12 sector and postsecondary institutions, parents, and community and private sector resources; and the need for the issue of minority student education to be framed as an urgent state policy concern. The report concludes with a brief description of WICHE's Exemplary Programs for College Bound Minority Students. Project STEP is included in this list. The report is primarily aimed at the postsecondary sector, outlining problems and strategies for improved academic performance and retention of minority students in colleges and universities. However, many of the excellent points contained in this report are equally applicable to the K-12 experience. Particularly relevant to prospective partnerships is a list of useful program features drawn from college and university outreach programs and community groups.

Olsen, L. (1988). ***Crossing the Schoolhouse Border: Immigrant Students and the California Public Schools.*** A California Tomorrow Policy Research Report. San Francisco, CA: California Tomorrow.

This report is unique in that it emphasizes the human and social difficulties which impede the educational advancement of immigrant children in California schools. The research includes evidence not only from educators and administrators, but from 360 structured in-depth interviews with immigrant students, aged 11-18. The report is replete with quotations from these students, capturing very effectively the emotional and social trauma and the physical violence that often pervades the immigrant school experience. Consequently the report emphasizes the need for a **comprehensive** approach to developing school structures and approaches which will assist **all** children to function effectively in a growingly diverse culture and to tolerate and cherish those who are different from themselves. The report gives specific resource information about programs and strategies that have been effective but stresses that most schools are not adequately prepared to integrate immigrant children into their academic curriculum, particularly in view of a critical shortage of bilingual teaching staff. Project STEP provides a model for the kind of comprehensive approach that a school/college partnership can provide to support districts and schools with a high enrollment of minority students. Given the severity of the social and educational problems outlined in this report, educators from all sectors must combine resources and skills using strategies such as academic partnerships to integrate the large numbers of immigrant children into the state educational system and provide them with access to educational opportunities.

Peters, T.J. and Waterman, R.H. ***In Search of Excellence: Lessons from America's Best-Run Companies.*** (1982). New York, NY: Warner Books.

On this book's cover, ***The Wall Street Journal*** describes it as "Exuberant and absorbing . . .one of those rare books on management that is both consistently thought-provoking and fun to read." The advice from the corporate world is particularly relevant as academic partnerships increasingly seek to involve the business sector in their endeavors. However, whether or not a partnership includes the business sector, this is an extremely useful, easy-to-read text for managers and leaders of potential partnerships. It outlines a set of specific organizational attributes that the authors found to characterize "excellent" American companies. Many of these attributes are directly applicable to academic partnerships, particularly ideas about the importance of developing an organizational "culture," of encouraging autonomy and innovation among task forces, of building a sense of pride and ownership among rank and file members, and of the overriding importance of developing a strong sense of core values understood by everyone within the organization.

Seeley, D.S. ***Education Through Partnership.*** (1981). An American Enterprise Institute Book. Cambridge, MA: Ballinger Publishing Company.

This book is part of a three-year study of "mediating structures": families, communities, voluntary associations and religious groups. The author argues that these groups generate and communicate meaning and values within society. Seeley calls for a restructuring of the schools in terms of a "partnership policy," which would bring these mediating structures, particularly the family, back into the schools and in the process reduce governmental and bureaucratic control. Seeley's argument, that education should be regarded altogether in terms of a partnership, serves as an interesting theoretic and philosophic validation for specific partnership efforts. Seeley argues persuasively, and with good support from social science research, that treating teachers, students and parents as real partners within schools will provide them with greater "voice" and "choice" and consequently inspire their loyalty and commitment to the educational process. Seeley's book reminds us of the importance of including the voice of parents and students in partnership efforts. He quotes the Carnegie Council on Children that American parents have a "new job" in "choosing, meeting, talking with, and coordinating with the experts, the technology, and the institutions that help bring up their children."

Sirotnik, K.A. and Goodlad, J.I., (1988). ***School-University Partnerships in Action.*** New York, NY: Teachers College Press.

Sirotnik and Goodlad's book provides an extremely useful and balanced introduction to the idea of school-university partnerships. Goodlad outlines a useful reference list of "minimum essential elements" of a successful partnership in terms of concept, purpose, agenda and structure. The literature regarding partnership terminology and experiences is reviewed. The longest section of the book analyzes a selected set of case histories of school-university partnerships which illustrate the important point that the shape of partnerships must be adapted to the needs and interests of specific partners. In the last section, Sirotnik outlines approaches to research and evaluation based on Goodlad's partnership paradigm. In doing so, he gives valuable recommendations about documentation and process tracing within a partnership. Goodlad concludes the book with a reflection on the problems that emerged in the case study partnerships and that can emerge in any school-university partnership.

The Task Force on Women, Minorities and the Handicapped in Science and Technology. Interim Report (1988). ***Changing America: The New Face of Science and Engineering.*** Washington, D.C.: U.S. Department of Education.

This report was compiled by a task force composed of members drawn from fifteen federal agencies and leaders in the private sector and education. The recommendations contained in the report are based on a series of public hearings held across the nation, and attended by leaders of the educational and private sectors between Fall 1987 and Spring 1988. The report argues that current educational strategies are failing to reproduce the workers needed to meet future demand in scientific and engineering fields. Consequently, not only is our position as a technological, economic and military leader being eroded but even our prospects for maintaining an advanced industrial society are being diminished. Meanwhile, by the year 2000, 85% of new entrants to the nation's workforce will be minorities and women. The report outlines a series of goals and activities designed to improve education in the areas of science and technology and to recruit women, minorities and handicapped people into these fields. One suggestion relevant to this handbook is to forge academic partnerships between institutions which have significant enrollments from underrepresented groups and departments of science and engineering at research universities.

Yount, R. (1985). ***Partnership for Excellence: School/College Collaboration and Building Teacher Education Systems Statewide.*** Washington, D.C.: Council of Chief State School Officers.

This book comprises a series of papers and panel presentations from the 1985 summer institute of the Council of Chief State School Officers. This institute focused on the enhancement of elementary and secondary education through school/college collaboration. Many papers emphasize the benefits of school/college collaboration for teacher preparation. Others discuss such topics as the organizational dynamics of school/university partnerships, the problems and nature of the high school-college transition and case studies of alternative school/college collaborative programs. This compilation of papers is thought provoking because it presents verbatim panel responses to the positions and experiences presented. Consequently the reader is provided with a variety of perspectives on the benefits and problems of academic partnerships from both the K-12 and the postsecondary sector.

BIBLIOGRAPHY

Atkin, Myron J. and Atkin, A. 1989. ***Improving Science Education Through Local Alliances.*** A Report to the Carnegie Corporation of New York. Santa Cruz, CA: Network Publications.

Bissell, J.S. (in press). "Success in Fostering Multimedia in K-12 and Higher Education: A Case Study." ***Productivity and Learning in the Visual Information Age.*** Alfred P.Sloan Foundation.

Bissell, J.S. October 28, 1989. "The Case Project in Educational Administration." Paper Presented at the Conference of the University Council for Educational Administration.

Bissell, J.S., Travers, J.R. and Beck R. 1982. "Measuring the Outcomes of Day Care." ***Learning from Experience: Evaluating Early Childhood Demonstration Programs.*** Washington, D.C.: National Academy Press.

Bissell, J.S., et al. 1980. "Evaluating Human Services Integration." ***Evaluation and Change.***

Bissell, J.S. February 1980. ***Program Evaluation as a Title VII Management Tool.*** Washington, D.C., U.S. Department of Education.

Boyer, E. 1985. "The Need for School-College Collaboration." ***Higher Education and National Affairs.*** Washington, D.C.: American Council on Education.

California Commission on Educational Quality. Report to the Governor. 1988. Sacramento, CA: Governor's Office.

Castruita, R. 1989. ***A Letter of Support for the Science 2000 proposal.***

Clark, E.D. 1975. "A Conceptual Basis for Collaboration." ***Emerging Concepts for Collaboration,*** Bulletin #40. Washington, D.C.: Association of Teacher Educators, 1-17.

Clark, E.D. August, 1986. ***School/University Relations: Partnerships and Networks Occasional Paper No. 2.***

Daly, W.T. 1985. ***College-School Collaboration: Appraising the Major Approaches*** (New Directions for Teaching and Learning, No. 24), San Francisco, CA: Jossey-Bass.

Davies, H.D. and Aquino, J.T.Fall 1985. "Collaboration in Continuing Professional Development." ***Journal of Teacher Education*** 26, No. 3 : 274-277.

DeBeavoise, W. 1986. "Collaboration: Some Principles of Bridgework." ***Educational Leadership.*** February 1986, 43, 5, 9-12.

Dewey, J. 1916. ***Democracy and Education: An Introduction to the Philosophy of Education*** . New York, NY: Macmillan Co.

Dewey, J. 1938. ***Logic: The Theory of Inquiry.*** New York, NY: Henry Holt and Co.

Galligani, D.J. 1987. ***Effective Relationships for School/College Partnerships: A Qualitative Evaluation of the Curriculum Enhancement Projects Participating in the California Academic Partnership Program 1984-1987.*** California State University Long Beach, CA: California Academic Partnership Program.

Gaudiani, C. and Burnett, D. 1986. ***Academic Alliances: A New Approach to School/College Collaboration.*** Washington, D.C.: American Association for Higher Education.

Gomez, M. 1983. ***Hearings Before the Subcommittee on Postsecondary Education of the Committee on Education and Labor House of Representatives.*** Washington, D.C.: 98th Congress, 1st Conference.

Gomez, M. October 31, 1984. ***Establishing Common Ground: School College Partnerships.*** A presentation to the Assembly Committee on Education, Santa Barbara, CA.

Gomez, M. 1989. ***UCI State of the Campus: 25 Years of Partnership.*** A presentation to the Regents, June 16, 1989.

Goodlad, J.I. 1984. ***A Place Called School: Prospects for the Future.*** New York, NY: McGraw-Hill.

Gross, T.L. 1988. ***Partners in Education: How Colleges Can Work with Schools to Improve Teaching and Learning.*** San Francisco, CA: Jossey-Bass.

Hathaway, W.E. March 1985. ***Models of School-University Collaboration: National and Local perspectives on Collaborations That Work.*** Chicago, IL: Paper presented for Symposium at the Annual Meeting of American Educational Research Association, (ED 253 973).

Havelock, R.G. 1973. ***The Change Agent's Guide to Innovation in Education.*** Englewood Cliffs, N.J.: Education Technology Publications.

Havelock, R., Huberman, M., Levinson, R., & Cox, P. 1982. ***School-university collaboration supporting school improvement.*** Cross-site analysis, Vol. 3. Washington, D.C.: American University, Knowledge Transfer Institute. (NIE Contract No. 400-79-0063).

Haycock, K. and Navarro, M. May 1988. ***Unfinished Business: Fulfilling Our Children's Promise.*** Oakland, CA: The Achievement Council.

Holmes Group. 1986. ***Tomorrow's Teachers: A Report of the Holmes Group.*** East Lansing, MI: Holmes Group, Inc.

Hord, S.M. February, 1986. "A synthesis of research on organizational collaboration." ***Educational Leadership.*** pp. 22-26.

Huberman, M. 1982. "Making Changes From Exchanges: Some Frameworks for Studying the Teachers' Centers Exchange." ***Networking on Purpose,*** edited by K.Devaney. San Francisco, CA: Far West Laboratory.

Intriligator, B.A. 1982. "Inter-Organizational Collaboration: A Strategy for Faculty Development and Renewal." ***Journal of Teacher Education.*** Sep./Oct. 1982: 14-17.

Lieberman, A. 1986. "Collaborative Research: Working With, Not Working On . . ." ***Educational Leadership,,*** February 1986a, 28-32.

Lieberman, A. 1986. "A Collaborative Work." *Educational Leadership,* February 1986b, 4-8.

Lillyman, Dr. William J. 1983. *Address to the Student Preparation Committee.* Office of the President--Universitywide. Dec. 19, 1983.

Lortie, D.C. 1977. *Networks and Organizational Rationality in American Public Schools.* Washington, D.C.: NIE.

Maeroff, G. 1983. *School and College Partnerships in Education.* Princeton, N.J.: The Carnegie Foundation for the Advancement of Teaching.

Martin, D.A., Mocker, D.W., Brown, N.C. 1986. *Joining Forces for Urban Youth: The NASULGC Urban University/Urban School Collaborative Program.* Washington D.C.: American Enterprise for Public Policy Research.

Miles, M. *On Networking.* Washington D.C.: National Institute of Education, Group on School Capacity for Problem-Solving.

National Commission on Excellence in Education. 1983. *A Nation at Risk.* Washington, D.C.: The Commission.

National Science Board Commission on Precollege Education in Mathematics, Science and Technology. 1983. *Educating Americans for the 21st Century.* Washington, D.C.: National Science Foundation.

Odell, M. and Mock, J., eds. 1989. *A Crucial Agenda: Making Colleges Work Better for Minority Students.* Boulder, CO: Western Interstate Commission for Higher Education.

Oliva, M. A. 1986. *Latino College Students.* New York, NY: Teachers College Press.

Olsen, L. 1988. *Crossing the Schoolhouse Border: Immigrant Students and the California Public Schools.* A California Tomorrow Policy Research Report. San Francisco, CA

Otterbourg, S.D. 1986. *School Partnerships Handbook.* New Jersey: Prentice Hall.

Parkay, F.W. "A School/University Partnership that Fosters Inquiry-Oriented Staff Development." ***Phi Delta Kappan,*** 67. 386-389.

Peters, T.J. Waterman, R.H. 1982. ***In Search of Excellence: Lessons from America's best-run companies.*** New York: Warner Books.

Quality Education for Minorities Project. Jan. 1990. ***Education that Works: An Action Plan for the Education of Minorities.*** Cambridge, MA.

Sarason, S. et al. 1977. ***Human Services and Resource Networks.*** San Francisco: Jossey-Bass.

Schon, D.A. 1977. ***Network-Related Intervention,*** Washington, D.C.: National Institute of Education.

Schopenhauer,A. 1816. ***World as Will and Idea.*** 1957 edition translated from German by Haldare, R.B and Kemp, J. London, UK: L.K. Paul Routledge.

Seeley, D.S. 1981. ***Education Through Partnership: Mediating Structures and Education.*** Cambridge, MA: Ballinger Publishing Co.

Shive, R.J. 1984. "School and University Partnerships: Meeting Common Needs." ***Improving College and University Teaching*** 32, No.3 (Summer 1984: 119-122).

Sirotnik, K.A. and Goodlad, J.I. 1988. ***School-University Partnerships in Action.*** New York, NY: Teachers College Press.

Sizer, T.R. 1984. ***Horace's Compromise: The Dilemma of the American High School.*** Boston, MA: Houghton Mifflin.

Smith, E.B., and J.I. Goodlad. 1966. "Promises and Pitfalls in the Trend Toward Collaboration." ***Partnership in Teacher Education.*** Washington, D.C.: American Association of Colleges for Teacher Education and The Association for Student Teaching.

Sosniak, L. 1989. ***Partnerships With A Purpose: A Case Study on Curriculum Development and Delivery Through School-College Collaboration.*** New York, NY: College Entrance Examination Board.

The Task Force on Women, Minorities and the Handicapped in Science and Technology. Interim Report 1988. ***Changing America: The New Face of Science and Engineering.*** Washington, D.C.: Department of Education.

Trubowitz, S. 1986. "Stages in the Development of School-College Collaboration." ***Educational Leadership*** 43, 5.

Trubowitz, S. Duncan, W., Fibkins, W., Longo, P. & Sarason, S.S. 1984. ***When a college works with a public school: A case study of school-college collaboration.*** Boston, MA: Institute for Responsive Education.

United States Department of Education. May, 1984. The Nation Responds: Recent Efforts to Improve Education. Washington D.C.: U.S. Government Printing Office.

University-wide Program Review Committee for Education. 1984. ***The role of the University of California in precollegiate education.*** Berkeley, CA: University of California.

Van de Water. 1988. ***The Governance of School-College Collaboratives: Lessons Learned from the College-Board's Educational Equality Project Models Program fore School-College Collaboration.*** New York, NY: The College Board.

Wilbur, F.P. 1981. "High School College Partnerships That Work." ***Educational Record.***

Wilbur, F. 1985. "School-College Partnerships." ***Journal of College Admissions,*** Summer 1985, 20-28.

Wilbur, F.P., Lambert, L.M., Young, M.J. 1988. ***School College Partnerships--A Look at the Major National Models.*** Reston: VA: National Association of Secondary School Principals.

Wu, P.C. 1985. "School Districts and Universities and Staff Development: Is It a Mixture That Will Work?" Paper presented at the National Staff Development Council Conference. Denver, CO: December 1985.

Yale-New Haven Teacher Institute. 1984. ***Teaching in America: The Common Ground.*** New York, NY: College Entrance Board, 8.

Yount, R. 1985. ***Partnership for Excellence: School/College Collaboration and Building Teacher Education Systems Statewide.*** Washington, D.C.: Council of Chief State School Officers.